THE WOMAN WITHOUT
A NUMBER

Iby Knill

Scratching Shed Publishing Ltd

First published by Scratching Shed Publishing Ltd in 2010
Fourth reprint November 2013
Registered in England & Wales No. 6588772.
Registered office:
47 Street Lane, Leeds, West Yorkshire. LS8 1AP

www.scratchingshedpublishing.co.uk

ISBN 978-0956478764

A catalogue record for this book is available from the British Library.

Typeset in Warnock Pro Semi Bold and Palatino

Printed and bound in the United Kingdom by
Charlesworth Press, Flanshaw Way, Flanshaw Lane,
Wakefield, WF2 9LP

For my grandchildren, Julia, James and Katarina

Acknowledgements

First and foremost, thanks are due to the late Keith Wicks, my supervisor on the MA course who cajoled, encouraged, pushed and pulled me through the trauma of writing this book. Thanks to my dear friends Carolyn Berry and Sheelagh Spinks who wrapped me in their love while I fought my way down into the painful past, which I had managed to bury for many years, and to Michael Cross and Steve Jarrett who gave me spiritual support when I was hitting rock bottom and floundering. Also to Elizabeth Baxter and Holyrood House which gave me the space and tranquillity needed to finish it. Then I put the manuscript away.

I had written it and that was the most important thing. I could not bear to look at it, to read it or revise it. Yet there was still much I had not included. Even today there are sections I cannot look at and experiences I could not bear to describe. Then along came my young, energetic, enthusiastic friend, Rachel Britton, who picked it up, read it, decided to give it its name and to become its champion. Eventually, I took a critical look at it and rewrote and rearranged it into its present form - more or less. Her enthusiasm and that of my friends and fellow-writers of the Leeds Writers' Circle persuaded me that it was worth publishing.

Thanks to all at Princesstv and to Frank Gardner of the BBC who believed in my story. Last, but not least, thanks to Phil Caplan of Scratching Shed Publishing who had the courage others didn't and decided to publish the story of the woman without a number.

And finally thanks to my children, Chris Knill and Pauline Kinch, who travelled some of the way with me, together with assurances that the past cannot hurt them or me any more.

Contents

If - I hadn't had doubts and thoughts about faith and beliefs
If - I had not enrolled on the MA course in Theology
If - one of the modules had not been 'Topics in Christianity'
If - one topic had not been 'Sin and Evil'
If - we had not constructed a sort of line of what was sin and what was evil
If - one of the students had not asked: 'Where along this line would you put the Holocaust?'
If - the tutor had not replied: 'Only a person who had been there could answer that.'
If - I hadn't felt compelled to say: 'But I was there.'
Then this book would not have been written.

PART ONE

1

*

Desperate Measures

The man and girl walked purposefully out of the village wheeling their bikes, a basket strapped to his two-wheeler. Once outside the walls they started to ride. He warned her not to put the light on and they rode along illuminated by the crescent moon which made the road appear brighter than the surrounding fields. After about an hour, they got off the bikes and wheeled them around to the back of a small bus shelter.

'They'll be safe here,' he whispered. 'I'll collect them when I get back.' He unstrapped the basket and produced two rough sacks that had holes slit in them for head and arms.

'We might have to crawl some of the way; we don't want to get too dirty. Keep low and do not make any noise, whatever happens,' he explained.

They put on the sacks. He stepped down into a ditch and she followed. Crouching low, they followed the line of the road until they saw, a little way ahead, a barrier across it and a hut by its side. A soldier was walking up and down behind the bar, a floodlight circle spotlighting the ground. They waited. And waited.

Eventually, a light came on in the hut. Then the door opened and a voice called.

'Hey, Janos, I have warmed up the coffee, come and have some.'

Looking up and down the road, Janos replied, 'I'm coming,' and went in.

The moon obligingly hid behind a cloud. The man waved her on urgently. They crawled out of the ditch, into the field and behind the hut into the next field and then back into a ditch, crawling as fast as possible to get away before Janos resumed his sentry duties.

After about thirty metres further, the man motioned her to stop. They had just crawled across no-man's-land, leaving Slovakia and now had to get into Hungary. And the moon had come out again. This was potentially the most dangerous part. The guards on the Slovak side were locals and the man knew them and had bribed one of them to get Janos in at the agreed time. Now they had to trust to luck and to the sketchy knowledge the man had acquired about the movements of the Hungarian border guards.

This was a new frontier. During the existence of Czechoslovakia the main arm of the Danube had formed the border between Czechoslovakia and Hungary and the large fertile island between there and the Little Danube was part of Slovakia. When, after the Munich agreement of 1938, Bohemia and Moravia - the Czech part - became a Nazi protectorate and the eastern Slovak side a puppet state, this island and some more land to the east was handed over to Hungary. This area included Kosice, the town in which the girl had been born, making the residents now citizens of Hungary. The Little Danube, which had been forded and bridged in many places, then became the border. Certain crossings were well guarded; others less so. In some cases only one side guarded the border.

The man told her later that the guard hut on the Hungarian side was only manned intermittently and that frequently, even when occupied, the guard slept at night. The local wine helped.

Again they waited. Eventually, the man motioned the girl to stay put while he crawled forward to within hearing distance of the hut. Nothing moved. She heard an owl hoot. Still nothing moved. There were no lights except some small red ones on the bar across the road.

The man crawled on. She lost sight of him in the darkness and was getting scared.

The owl hooted twice, then once. The signal! The road was clear. She crawled, as before – ditch, field, behind the hut, field, ditch barely daring to breathe. She bumped into the man.

'We're through. We'll be all right now. It's better if we stay in the ditch for a little while longer, but we shall be able to get on to the road soon,' he said.

The little longer was probably the best part of half a mile. They came to a crossroad, got up, took off the sacks, wiped their boots with them and then discarded them in the ditch. Trying to look like normal village people, she walking behind the man and carrying the basket, they moved in the early morning light towards the railway station for the local train to take them to Komarom.

It was so early she thought they would be the only people at the station and, therefore, rather conspicuous. But, as they got nearer, she heard murmuring and chirping, like a swarm of bees accompanying a flock of starlings. She realised that they would have company.

The station platform was thronged with women – and a few men – in their native costume of skirts over skirts over skirts, covered by a voluminous apron. Instead of the usual blouse with its richly embroidered sleeves and neckband, the women wore plain white shirts. A few even had shirts in gingham checks. Many of them wore a plain waistcoat, laced up the front, not the embroidered and beaded ones which they wore to church and on high days and holidays. A large square of material, printed mainly with red roses, covered their heads. It was big enough to cross over the front and to be tied at the back. A few of the younger women were dressed like the girl: boots and coat and a kerchief on their heads, tied either under the chin or at the back of the neck. They all had large baskets containing live hens, or eggs or root vegetables. A few contained small items of lace or embroidery. All of them were hoping to sell their goods in Komarom because it was market day there. The girl realised that the man had fixed things well. Her small basket, covered with a gingham cloth, could have contained eggs or lace, but held all her belongings – her handbag with her birth certificate, which showed that she had been born in Kosice, called Kassa by the Hungarians. In its comments it stated that her father was an officer, a Hungarian national. Although she did not have the obligatory identity card, she hoped that this would carry some weight. It made no mention of the fact that he had resigned Hungarian citizenship, once he was no longer liable for service in the Reserve and was now a Czechoslovak citizen, as was his whole family.

The man went and bought tickets. When the train arrived there was some pushing and shoving. Most of the women knew each other, travelling in groups and wanted to be together in the same compartment. Those nimblest on their feet grabbed the window seats and spread out their skirts to keep places for their friends. Except for one coach, all the others were third class, with slatted wooden benches like garden seats and, depending on their girth and the number of skirts they wore, each side could accommodate up to five people. The man and the girl managed to squeeze themselves on to two seats on the corridor side of a compartment.

The little train stopped at more stations. It had not been empty when it got to the station where they got on but it gradually became so full that people were standing between the benches and sitting on each other's laps. The corridors were a heaving mass of people and baskets. She could hear the ticket collector shouting some distance away, asking to be let through but all he got in reply was some good-natured repartee, asking him to climb over their heads; they would help him along. Some of the baskets were now on people's heads as there was no space on the floor, so he stayed put. His presence on the train wasn't really necessary, since in Komarom one had to show one's ticket on leaving the platform. Travelling without a ticket was not really a practical proposition.

Once they arrived at Komarom, all the women made a rush for the exit and moved like a wave towards the market. The man and the girl lagged behind, they had nothing to sell.

'Breakfast?' he asked.

She nodded. They went into the station restaurant. This felt relatively safe, in spite of the large number of police, soldiers and border guards at and around the station. Her Hungarian was fluent and free of any accent so they could talk freely and without fear of identification. The man ordered coffee and rolls. Having eaten, they still had more than two hours to wait for the train to Budapest. The man thought they were bound to be asked questions if they loitered around the station and suggested they went for a walk. Neither of them knew either Komarno or Komarom.

Komarom railway station was south of the river and had always been Hungarian. They wandered along the riverbank, came to the bridge and were about to cross it when they realised that on both sides were border guards and that the bridge itself was a no-man's-land. They also noticed that people were allowed to leave this side and get onto the bridge but that anyone trying to come off the bridge had their papers carefully scrutinised. Not a risk they could take, so they continued to walk. They passed a hotel. The man stopped.

'We could pass an hour here.'

'Here?' she asked. 'Why?'

'You know', he said, making the gesture indicating sex.

'Oh, no! Whatever are you thinking of?' she replied, turning round and starting to walk back quickly towards the station. The very idea! Whatever had put such a thought into his head?

'I meant no harm,' he said, 'I just thought it would pass the time.'

She was too aghast to reply. How did he dare! She was not yet of an age to have a cynical attitude towards sex – that would come later.

They went back to the station; she was too perturbed to reply to him when he remarked on this or that. Just before they got to the station he said, 'I'm sorry, don't tell your parents.'

'There's nothing to tell', she replied, adding bitterly, 'I might never see them again, anyhow.'

THE JOURNEY TO BUDAPEST passed in silence. She had made the trip many times before, both with her parents and on her own. They arrived there, at the West Station and had to find their way to aunt Bella's home on József Körút, the Ring Road. Her father had given her detailed instructions when she had travelled on her own to Budapest a couple of years before, which tram to take and where to change. The last part was on foot, she remembered those instructions.

They found Number 21, took the stairs not the lift to the third floor and rang the bell. It was about 6pm. After a short delay aunt Bella opened the door.

The man said, 'I have brought Iby, your niece.' He assumed that she had been warned of their arrival. By this time everyone knew what was happening to Jews in any country over which the Germans had control. Hungary, having agreed to support Germany's war effort and place its own dictatorship under Admiral Horty, was more valuable to Germany as an ally than as an occupied territory. Aunt Bella was reluctant to let them in. The man explained that he had to go back immediately; he had to catch the train home, that the arrangements only involved getting the girl to Budapest.

Eventually she let them into the kitchen but was adamant, she was not going to have the girl there – it was too dangerous; aunt Bella would be fined or even imprisoned if they found that she was harbouring someone who had entered the country illegally. That the girl's life was likely to be forfeited if she went back did not interest her at all. While the man and the girl were still trying to get her to change her mind, the doorbell rang.

They all froze – there was no way anyone could know that they were here. The bell rang again and they heard a voice call out: 'It's me, wake up aunt Bella, let me in!' It was Marton, Iby's cousin, the son of aunt Theresa, aunt Bella's elder sister. Theresa had died a couple of years earlier and, as Aunt Bella had no children, Marton kept an eye on her, checking every day that everything was in order. She was now in her forties and had friends – mainly men friends, as Iby discovered later. 'Marton will agree with me,' said aunt Bella, as she went to open the door.

The Woman Without A Number

Hardly had Marton, my glamorous blond cousin entered the kitchen when I blurted out, 'I don't know what's to become of me! Aunt Bella won't let me stay and John can't take me back. Even if he did manage to do that it would be the end of me. What am I going to do?'

Marton turned to aunt Bella. 'There is no question of Iby being sent back,' he said forcefully. 'How could you even think of that? Why can't Iby stay here? You haven't a maid at the moment. She could use her room and you could say she is your new maid.'

'That's far too dangerous,' Bella replied. 'Iby's been here before and someone in the building is bound to remember her. She just has to go back.' All looked down, except John. We did not dare to look into each other's eyes. I clenched my fists in my lap and tried not to tremble.

Marton lifted up his head, 'I know, she can come and stay with me.'

'With you?' queried Bella. 'You are a bachelor, living on your own. What would people say?'

'Does that really matter? All that's important is that they should not know she is here illegally. I don't think they will suspect that as Iby would not be the first woman to stay overnight. I'll sort out something for the daytime. He looked at his watch, 'I have to go back to work, I don't finish until ten. Surely she can stay here until then? Nobody knows she is here.'

Even aunt Bella could no longer protest.

John had taken such a dislike to aunt Bella that he would not even accept a cup of coffee. He left in a hurry to get the train back. The following year John helped my parents, my brother Tomy, cousin Magda and my grandmother across the border. He was well paid, but he took risks for us. Mother told me after the war that the valuables which had been given to him and Mariska to hide were returned in

18

immaculate conditions after the war. That is why I have photographs and papers about my childhood. John could not know whether any of us would survive the war, but he kept faith. Some others didn't. His wife Mariska had been our cook before she married John.

After John had left, aunt Bella asked me whether I was hungry. I had eaten nothing since that roll and coffee in Komarom and was very hungry.

'I've got some soup,' she said doubtfully. Aunt Bella's lack of culinary skills were well known in the family but this nondescript soup and bread were nectar and ambrosia to a hungry teenager.

So far, everything had taken place in the kitchen.

'Where's your luggage?' asked aunt Bella.

'This is it.' I indicated the basket. Aunt Bella shook her head and clicked her tongue.

What did I have with me? I wore dark brown boots and had a pair of matching shoes in the basket. My tweed coat had a warm lining and I had a cap of the same material and a kerchief. I wore a skirt and jacket and a warm blouse and there was another blouse, knickers, stockings, a nightie, toothbrush, soap and a small towel. Beside a handbag, I also had warm gloves, two handkerchiefs, comb, brush, lipstick and a powder compact. I had nothing by which I could be identified except my birth certificate and, for emergencies, two gold coins sewn into the hem of the coat in lieu of the usual lead disks. My purse had some Hungarian money, but, having paid for the tram, only *filers*, Hungarian coinage, were left.

'How will you manage with so little?' asked aunt Bella. I could only shrug and look at her silently. What choice did I have?

'You can sew?' She asked. I nodded, I had no idea at the time how useful that skill would be to me time and again.

The Woman Without A Number

She went out and came back with a length of brown silky fabric. 'You might be able to make something out of this. It's not really my colour.' Aunt Bella was so drab that brown was certainly not her colour.

I spent the next hours sitting alone in the kitchen while aunt Bella had to do some business in her office but we did not have a lot to say to each other anyway.

It had been an eventful week. How had it started? What did I know about aunt Bella?

At this time she was a widow. Her husband had been Mor Meitner and in the film business. I remembered spending a marvellous week with them one summer when I was about fourteen while the Budapest Film Festival was on and having complimentary tickets to at least three films every day. Uncle Mor was the distributor for UFA, a German film company in Hungary and in his studio German films were dubbed into Hungarian. During another summer I did the voice-overs which I thought very exciting and glamorous. I fondly recalled, when I was no more than ten, having as a birthday present a home movie outfit with a selection of short films – not only cartoons. That was a very special gift for a child in the early 1930's.

After Uncle Mor died, aunt Bella tried to carry on at the studio as best she could. Off and on she had temporary business partners and one of them was also now her lover; my presence in aunt Bella's apartment would have been awkward for them. That was also the reason why she preferred not to have a maid at this time.

2

*

Growing Up Fast

Marton was indeed back by ten. 'Have you had something to eat?' he asked.

'I gave her some soup,' said aunt Bella.

'Do you think that's enough?' asked Marton.

Aunt Bella was thin and small like a sparrow.

'Did you have lunch?' He asked me.

I shook my head.

'Come on, girl, let's go. I'll see you tomorrow,' to aunt Bella.

'Wouldn't it be safer, if you didn't come while Iby is with you?' she replied.

Marton shrugged his shoulders: 'If that's what you want.'

I never found out what Marton really did for a living. He drove a large black car 'as a job', so he said and I think that he must have been some sort of semi-official driver for a government department because he certainly knew some unusual and influential people, as I found out later.

His car was outside.

The Woman Without A Number

'You'd better get in the back like a passenger and let me have your basket. We'll have something to eat and then we'll go home. Pretend you're my girlfriend.'

Although I was reasonably familiar with some parts of Budapest, I did not know the cellar restaurant with its smoky atmosphere to which Marton took me. It looked slightly unsavoury – and probably was. Marton ordered us the ubiquitous paprika chicken with little dumplings and cucumber salad, a glass of wine for himself and a spritzer for me. My insides, which had been in a tight knot since the previous evening, started to unwind. Someone was now looking after me. But when the gypsy violist came to our table and started to play *Csak egy kislany van a vilagon* [There is only one little girl in the world] which was the tune my father had sung and played to me since babyhood, it took all my strength not to burst into tears. It had been a traumatic day and I really did not need her serenade. Nor was the day over yet, not by a long way.

Marton realised that I was upset, waved the gypsy off, paid the bill, took me by the elbow and led me back to the car. Once outside, I did burst into tears. Marton wrapped his arms around me and shushed me, as one would a child – which I was.

Before we got to the block of flats where Marton lived, he explained: 'I have brought women back to the flat before, so nobody will think it odd that you are with me but they always leave, usually in the morning. In the daytime you must be absolutely quiet. Keep out of sight of the windows, don't turn on the tap, do not flush the toilet – in other words, pretend that the flat is empty. Most importantly, do not answer the door or go near it. People do look through the letterbox if they ring the bell and nobody answers.'

Marton's flat in Garay Street had been his mother's originally. When she died, her younger son Laci, who had just married, took with him the house linen, most of the crockery and cutlery and other moveable items, leaving Marton the flat itself and its old bulky furniture.

The block, like most in Budapest at that time, was built in the shape of a hollow square with staircases going up to a gallery on each floor from which opened the doors of the individual flats. The windows of the rooms faced the street, the kitchen window opened onto the gallery.

His flat was on the third floor and there was no lift. The front door opened straight into the kitchen, which was like a wide corridor. At the other end of it, a door led into the living room and from there to the only bedroom. There was no bathroom. A door on the right side of the kitchen led to the toilet, which also had a low-level cold-water sink, used for filling buckets.

Marton undid the three locks on the door and ushered me in. He did not switch on the light. He locked the door behind us and put on the chain.

'Don't move,' he said.

I stayed still while he went into the sitting room, which was lit by the street lamp just outside the window. He drew the curtains, went into the bedroom, and closed them there as well. He then came for me, took my hand, let me into the sitting room, closed the door behind me and turned on the light – a solitary bulb hanging from the ceiling.

Only next day, in daylight, did the full horror of the place strike home. That it was dusty was understandable but it was truly dirty, neglected and unlived-in, in truth, a dump. I had never seen a place like it before.

Marton looked around – perhaps seeing the place clearly with my eyes for the first time and said sheepishly: 'Well, I only sleep here.'

'In here?' I asked and moved towards the bedroom.

That room was possibly even worse. How could Marton,

who was always clean and immaculately dressed, live or even sleep in this mess?

There was a huge, old-fashioned bedstead but one side had only wooden slats in it. The two mattresses had been put on top of each other – no doubt to make it more comfortable. The bed had not been made and the sheets did not look particularly clean. In those days, all bed linen was white; these were grey and stained, the pillowcases equally discoloured. Clothing covered every surface, the mirror in the wardrobe door was opaque with dust and finger marks and it was cold, freezing cold.

'Where am I going to sleep?' I whispered.

'Oh, don't worry, I'll sort it out, there's plenty of stuff,' replied Marton.

He heaved the bedding clear, then pulled off the mattresses and redistributed the wooden slats. He put both mattresses back. 'It should hold,' he said.

He then opened the chest of drawers, presumably to look for sheets.

'I don't know but it looks as if Laci has taken more than his share. This will have to do for now.'

He found a grey blanket, which he put on one mattress, replacing the repulsive bedding on the other one. He went into the sitting room and came back with a couple of gaudy embroidered cushions. He threw them on what was to be my bed.

'I'll get a drink, while you get into bed. Want some?'

I shook my head – by now I was past speaking.

I quickly undressed and put on my nightdress. I then had second thoughts and put my warm blouse back on top. I rolled myself up in the blanket and put my coat over it.

Sheer exhaustion made me fall asleep immediately.

I did not hear Marton come in or go to bed – or indeed anything until a chink of light between the drawn curtains made me realise that it was daytime – and that I was on my own in the flat.

Washing presented a problem as Marton had told me not to run any water. I wet a corner of my small towel under the dripping kitchen tap, wiped my face and hands and got dressed. Marton had left the curtains drawn so the only light came from the kitchen. The kitchen window had a grimy lace curtain to give some privacy. Marton had left a cup of coffee on the table. It was cold by now. There was a note. 'Put the chain quietly on the door. I shall be back lunchtime. I shall unlock the two locks and tap twice on the door for you to take the chain off.'

I looked for food. There was a bag of sugar, coffee, salt, paprika, but no bread, biscuits or anything that was remotely edible. The kitchen sink was full of dirty cups and glasses. It looked as if they had been there forever, maybe even since aunt Theresa's death. The toilet next door smelled, I had been told not to flush it but I had to use it.

I picked up the cold, bitter coffee, added some sugar, went into the sitting room, sat on the corner of a chair and sipped it. Not only was the coffee chilled but so was I. It felt as if a dank miasma was permeating the flat. I wrapped my coat and the blanket tightly around me and crawled into the corner of the disreputable-looking, sagging settee. It seemed that midday would never come.

When I heard the two locks and the two taps I crawled on all fours to the door, pulled back the chain and sat back on my heels. I did not feel that I had the strength to do anything else.

I don't think Marton had any idea of what he let himself in for when he agreed to shelter me. Nor had I. But he had been shopping. There was bread, butter, salami and cheese and even a couple of apples.

'Soap?' I whispered.

'Soap?' he replied.

I nodded and just made a sweeping gesture across the flat.

'Hmm, I see what you mean. By God, it is cold in here. I never realised it. But then, I am never here in the daytime and often not even at night. I'll do something about that.'

He was as good as his word. When he came home in the evening he brought a single bar electric fire and also a pair of new white sheets.

That evening - and every evening - we went out to eat in different places, he seemed to be known everywhere and I wondered why and how.

Marton had never regularly had food in the flat. His routine meant that he went for breakfast to a coffee house, had lunch wherever he happened to be and ate out also in the evening. It was important that he should maintain this normality. Usually he was gone from early in the morning and I was then left to my own devices for the rest of the day.

We worked out that if the curtains at the front were not quite drawn – there were no nets – I could crawl around the rooms below window level and stand up when out of the line of sight, provided I had no shoes on. I had to keep the door closed between the kitchen and the sitting room, so the light should not show my shadow in the kitchen. One of the panes at the bottom of the kitchen window was cracked and Marton masked it with newspaper. Nobody could look in now and there was still sufficient light in the daytime. Evenings on my own would be more difficult, I would just have to stay in the dark.

After a few days I realised that there was an hour or so in the morning when the women from the adjoining flats, on both sides, went shopping – usually together. Housework was not something I liked but the situation demanded drastic action. While they were out I managed, over the next days, to wash the kitchen floor, the dishes and to clean the surfaces. That also gave me a chance to have a proper wash and to wash my smalls, drying them in front of the electric fire. I tried to be as quiet as possible so that the people in the flat above or below did not hear me, I hoped they were shopping en masse.

Marton was adamant that I was not to touch any of his clothes. He bundled them into the wardrobe, locked it and took away the key. I wondered what he had to hide?

I had done what I could to make the place comparatively clean. I could not beat the dust out of the settee nor brush the curtains or clean the windows. There was now little to do and nothing to read. For someone like me, who could not live without books, that was not easy.

So I sat in front of the one-bar fire, day-dreaming. I had not realised how my whole existence became centred upon that single orange, glowing bar while waiting for Marton to come home in the evenings, until the day when the fire blew.

As the flat got colder and colder I wrapped myself in my coat and then in the blanket and retreated to a corner of the room, which could not be overlooked from anywhere. A wave of despair hit me. I started to shiver and rock and weep silently.

What was to become of me? Would I stay here forever, a prisoner to all intents and purposes? Why ever had I come? Could anything be any worse?

I lost all track of time. I must have withdrawn completely into myself. Not only did I forget to put the chain on the door, I never even heard Marton unlocking it. I did not hear his two taps sign, I just sat in the corner, rocking, shivering and letting the tears stream down my face. That was where Marton found me.

He had panicked when I had not responded to his knocks. He unlocked the third lock and had rushed in. On finding me still there he went quickly to re-lock the door, picked me up bodily, sat me on his knees and tried to rub my hands that felt like ice. I fell towards him, the tears continuing to flow and I could not stop my teeth from chattering.

He carried me to the bed, piled all the bedding from both on me – and still I shivered. He got in beside me, wrapped his arms around me trying to warm me, to stop the shivering. He rocked me in his arms, stroked my hair, kissed me and whispered endearments.

I don't know how it happened, he was kissing me gently and I nestled closer – then suddenly there was an urgency, an excruciating need - my despair and his desperation to help me enveloped us.

I don't think either of us realised what was happening – perhaps Marton felt that there was only one way left to warm me, to reassure me.

When it was over we drew apart and looked at each other in amazement. He put his finger on my lips to stop me speaking, kissed me gently on the top of my head and rocked me to sleep.

WHEN I WOKE IN the morning and instinctively reached over towards Marton, he wasn't there. Then I heard movement – Marton had lit the fire in the sitting room. He had not gone to work. Time had passed in such an odd way – how many days had I been here?

I wrapped the blanket around me and went into the living room. Marton was hunkered down in front of the fire, getting it going.

'It's Sunday. Our neighbours have gone to church and then they will visit family. They won't be in all day so we can talk. There's lots of hot water in the kitchen.'

I lifted the tin bath off the wall, filled it with water, closed the door between the kitchen and the sitting room and washed from head to toe. What a relief! Marton must have been shopping before he came home – brown paper bags were on the table.

When I was dressed I went back into the sitting room, I put my back to the stove waiting for warmth to seep through, but the stove had not been alight long enough and it was barely lukewarm. As if by consent, neither of us mentioned what had happened the previous day. I could not have talked about it to save my life and only half believed it. Possibly I had imagined it, perhaps I had dreamt it; maybe it had not happened.

Marton had gone to the kitchen and came back with a tray of bread, salami, butter, jam and a pot of coffee.

'Come and eat. We have to talk.'

'It's just not possible for you to stay locked up here day after day. In any case, I do not know how long I shall be allowed to stay. I have been informed that I'll be called up for Labour Service.'

'Labour Service?'

'I'll explain that later. I have spoken to people. This evening we are meeting somebody. If he thinks that you are reliable, you'll become part of the set-up. Don't ask me to explain but you'll have something to do in the daytime. As long as I am here you will spend the nights here – I will have acquired a 'not quite' occasional girl friend. When I have to go, you will stay with a family who will know who you are and will protect you. It all depends on whether things work out this evening. If they don't, I'll have to think of something else.'

'You mean – strangers? Can't I stay here?'

'No, the authorities know that I live on my own. When I go they'll seal the flat – or put someone else into it. It would not be possible to keep it for you on your own.'

The Woman Without A Number

'Yesterday ...?' I ventured.

'It just happened. It does sometimes but it doesn't mean anything has changed. I promised to look after you and I'll keep my promise – as far as I am able to do so. Do not fall in love with me or anything like that. We have always liked each other but, remember, these are dangerous times. Neither of us may have much time and falling in love is a luxury we can ill afford.'

The warning was appropriate. I was very young, malleable, susceptible, insecure, lonely and fearful – I could easily have fallen for him, or had I already? Nicky, my first boyfriend, my first love, was in another country, in another life. In a life which was over.

I spent the morning tidying; Marton was not domesticated but then in 1942 nobody expected a man to do anything around the house. While I was moving around the room, Marton explained to me what the situation was in Hungary, about the call-up to Labour Service which had been received by most Jewish men below fifty, that there were laws to punish people who harboured refugees who had entered the country illegally, that it was essential that a different, but not too different identity was arranged for me, one which would show that I was not Jewish. He would get me an ID card, once he knew where I was going to live, because it had to have the permanent place of residence on it.

He was following me around the room, getting in my way as I tidied. I kept on evading him, trying not to look at him.

Eventually he caught my arm and said, 'Iby, all this is very important, why don't you sit down so that I can talk to you properly? I have brought some newspapers. You really should read them. You must know what is happening here. In your new identity you have to be a girl of Budapest but not one of those who is not interested in anything but clothes and fashion. You have to know what goes on.'

In spite of what he had said about last night, which confirmed that I had not imagined it; in spite of all my misgivings, I felt a heightened awareness of him as a man, rather than as my cousin and I did not want him to notice this. He held my arm and with the other hand he lifted my chin so that I could not avoid looking at him. My eyes gave me away.

'Oh, no, oh, my God,' he whispered.

Our lovemaking that day and all the nights thereafter was always sad, as if each time we were saying goodbye to each other – and that was really the case because from that evening on I was as involved, as he was, in what could be deemed, 'activities contrary to the national interest' and each night could have been our last.

3

*

Found Out

That evening we did not go to the type of eating place Marton and I had been frequenting. We joined an elderly, elegant couple in one of the more fashionable restaurants.

Marton introduced me, 'This is Iby.'

Dr Marki lifted my hand in the gesture of kissing it, as was usual at that time in Hungary. The lady, who throughout the evening never said a word, nodded and smiled. Mrs Marki, Gabriella, as I called her later, was deaf and dumb, yet very beautiful, dignified and very kind.

The usual gypsy music provided suitable background noise, ensuring that our talk was not overheard. A meal was ordered and served.

Dr Marki asked me about my education, what languages I spoke, what my hobbies were, what kind of music I liked, whether I played a musical instrument and to what degree of proficiency, what books I had read and liked. He began by saying that he really only wanted to know about me – he did not want to hear or know anything about my family, friends or background. 'I need to know you, but it is very important for your family and friends that I should not know anything whatsoever about them.' His questions were probing but I had no problem answering.

His final question was; 'Do you have a boyfriend or lover?'

I looked at Marton. He looked straight back at me without any expression on his face. He had warned me to stick completely to the truth in all my answers. Were he and I lovers? In the actual sense yes but if Marton had been asked he would probably have said no. We found comfort in each other and that was a different kind of relationship.

'Not any more,' I said, 'he's...'

'No, do not tell me anything about him' Dr Marki interjected.

'Are you a virgin?'

Again I looked at Marton. He seemed to shake his head slightly.

'No,' I whispered.

'Good,' said Dr Marki.

'Yes,' he said, turning to Marton. 'Virgins can present problems.'

Marton sighed as if he had been holding his breath throughout this interrogation.

Dr Marki turned to me, 'Tomorrow morning at nine be in St John's church on Andrassy Street. When you enter, remember to dip the fingers of your right hand into the stoop and to cross yourself. Go to the fourth row of seats on the left and kneel. On the left you will see some confessionals. You understand?'

I nodded.

He turned to Marton. 'Leave Iby at the end of the street to make her own way to the church. Get a street map and cut out the page on which the church is. Give Iby that page.'

He turned to me. 'Stay in the pew, as near as you can to

the confessional. When the priest comes out he'll be wearing a white robe. Watch through which door he goes out. Count to ten after he has gone through the door, then follow him.'

He signalled the waiter for the bill to be brought, paid and they left. Marton and I followed shortly.

I had not been given the opportunity to ask anything of Dr Marki and was also too awed by him to do so. So I was bursting to ask questions of Marton.

As soon as we got outside I started. 'Can you tell me …'

'Not here, not now, nor in the car.,' he responded tersely. 'We'll walk the last part, then you can ask your questions.'

As we started to walk Marton said, 'There is really not a lot I am allowed to tell you, except that Dr Marki has agreed to take you on. You will be told what to do, where to go, whom to meet, what to wear. Never ask why; just do it. If you feel that you are asked to do something you cannot or do not wish to do, say so straight away. If you agree to do something you must carry it out, you cannot step back mid-way. Get a good night's sleep, you'll start a new life tomorrow.'

'And you?' I ventured.

'I'll be around as long as they let me. You are going to be my official girl friend.'

Next morning Marton and I did as instructed. I followed the priest through the door. He was standing with his back to a small window.

'How did you get here?' he asked.

'I walked,' I replied, 'I had a map.'

'Can I see it?' I passed him the page.

'Just one page?'

'Yes.'

'You are …?'

'Iby.'

'You are Jewish?'

34

'Yes, but I believe that my father was baptised in 1932, because ...'

'No, do not tell me. We must always ensure that we do not know any unnecessary information about any of us. It is safer. Were you religious at home? Do you know a lot about the Bible? Have you read it?' he queried.

'I only know stories, really,' I replied. 'When we did religion in the High School we made comparisons between Moses, Jesus and Marx.'

Religion had rested lightly on me in my childhood. Most of my school friends had been Christians, I knew that they were baptised and later confirmed and that they were not subject to the many laws and rules Jews were supposed to obey. We had been, what was the term? Assimilated.

'How interesting,' he said dryly. 'But if you are to live here and be safe you cannot remain Jewish. You understand that?'

I nodded.

'One can be baptised without having to undergo a course of instruction, if it is a matter of life and death. I consider that this is the case with you. But I would be easier in my heart if I knew whether you believed in God and in good and evil.'

'I wholeheartedly believe in them and that God watches over me.' I stressed.

'That's good enough for me.'

Father Andreas put both hands firmly on my head – I was kneeling – held them there for what seemed to me some time then dipped his right hand in a small bowl of water and made the sign of the cross on my forehead.

'I will record your baptism in the register of this church but not as of today. I am certain to find a gap at the bottom of a page some years ago, say in 1938.'

My sixth sense felt that there was something wrong – I had not been in Budapest in that year. In those days you had to register with the police if you were visiting from abroad – would anyone check?

Perhaps I should have said something but I didn't and that small matter was later instrumental in bringing down the whole carefully constructed edifice of 'resistance' work of which I was now part.

'You need to know something about me,' he continued. 'I am Father Andreas; I am a Dominican monk and father confessor to Madame Horty.' Admiral Horty was the Head of the Hungarian Government at that time

'I will also be your father confessor. You will be able to tell me anything you want and I promise that - even at the cost of my life - nobody will ever know what you have told me. If you are in serious trouble or are arrested, ask for me and they will let me come to you.'

He handed me two slim books.

'It will be useful for you to familiarise yourself with these,' he went on. 'One is the New Testament and the other a book of prayers.'

He handed me a small box. 'There is a rosary in here. Keep it with you always, in your handbag but not in the box. If you are in trouble and it should fall out of your bag it could prevent awkward questions. When we meet in future you have to greet me in the appropriate way. You'll bob down, I'll stretch out my hand and you kiss the ring on my hand. If I then put my hand on your head and say, 'God bless you, my child', it means that we are not alone or that we are in danger and we have to be very careful. Now – go with God, my child.'

'Where?' I asked, bewildered.

He indicated a point on the map.

'First floor. Ask to see Gabriella. Look now carefully at the map, so that you should know your way there. Never carry a map, as that would show that you do not know

Budapest. Also, you are a blonde. There are not many blonde girls in Budapest. Keep your hair covered unless you are told otherwise. Above all, do not be conspicuous, unless you want to be noticed.'

I saw Father Andreas quite often after that. He was a tower of strength and even when he could not come to me when I did eventually ask for him, I knew that I was in his thoughts and prayers.

I made my way to the home of Gabriella, Dr Marki's wife, to become her official companion. Gabriella was an expert in lip reading and I soon learned that skill as well as signing. She was fluent in English, as was I, and when we were in the presence of others we would lip-read in English, so that strangers could not even accidentally understand us.

During the next weeks I found out that my role was to be a messenger, or to create a diversion or to act as a honey trap – in between spending time with Gabriella, who was an exceedingly intelligent and delightful person. The Markis had two daughters, one of whom had died as a child, the other was now studying medicine.

I must have been in Budapest about three weeks, when one evening Marton arrived with a large suitcase.

'Don't ask me how this got here, I have no idea, but Aunt Bella phoned me to tell me that this had arrived for you.'

I opened it. My mother had sent me my clothes – or certainly enough of them to last me for some time. I never found out how she had managed to arrange it but then mother was a marvel of efficiency and ingenuity, who kept her cards close to her chest.

Over the next weeks I got to know the fleshpots of Budapest – the thermal baths on Margaret's Island, the various tea dances in the top hotels, the expensive cafes. I went wherever I was sent.

I can recall one particular occasion when I was

despatched to meet two young men near the Western Station. They were standing at the second lamppost – as I was told they would be. On walking towards them, one lit both their cigarettes, then shook the matchbox and shrugged his shoulders. As instructed, I took a cigarette out of my bag and approached them, asking for a light. The taller one took out the matchbox, shook it again and offered me the box. I opened it – it contained three matches. That was the sign. I lit my cigarette and handed the box back.

'You're waiting?' I queried.

'Yes, Sophia.'

'Come.'

I linked my arms into theirs and, walking between them, looked out for Marton's car. He passed us and stopped after the next crossroads. I motioned the two men into the car and waved them good-bye. Later on I found out that they were British airmen who had bailed out of their plane and were being taken 'along the line' to Yugoslavia to return to Britain.

On another occasion, I was told to go to a concert and to get the signature of the conductor afterwards. 'See whether you can make a date with him. Get him to meet you on the Fisherman's Bastion tomorrow, at three.' That was the first of many meetings I had with him and he gradually became involved in the movement. However, his endeavours to get me to sleep with him were not rewarded. He tried very hard, was delightful company, but I had my excuse ready. 'You are married and I would never sleep with a married man,' I frequently informed him. When at one meeting he said, 'Surely I deserve something for what I am doing?' Dr Marki decided that a different contact would be set up and that I should not meet him any more.

It was towards the end of April 1942 that Marton was called up to do Labour Service. We said goodbye to each other. He was convinced that, being young, strong and fit, he was in no danger. He promised to write to me at Dr Marki's address – and I believed it. However, I had no letters and heard after the war that he had frozen to death on the retreat from Russia. I was also told, in confidence, that he had made a will leaving everything to me. By this time I had realised how fragile life was and that I now had to depend entirely on strangers. Did I realise the dangerous game I was playing with my 'resistance' work? I don't think so. Did I find it exciting? Not really. I knew I was living on borrowed time, had no contact with my family and never thought about the future.

I now moved into Dr Marki's home and became part of his household as Gabriella's companion. Father Andreas visited Gabriella once a week – he was her father confessor. He had learned sign language and he also found time to talk to me, to spend time with me.

My needle again proved useful. I sewed for Gabriella, repaired the household linen and also made up the brown silk Aunt Bella had given me. Dr Marki thought that it should be an evening dress with a deep cleavage. In that dress, with my throaty voice and a long cigarette holder I could give a passable imitation of Marlene Dietrich singing 'Lilli Marlene'. On some nights, when told to do so, I took a taxi to a certain nightclub and sang. My repertoire was limited – and I was always told which of the songs I should sing. It was either the French 'J'attendrai' or 'Lilli Marlene' or 'My Bonny Lies Over the Ocean' in English and one or two Hungarian folksongs. The songs were obviously signals – I was never told what for and had realised by this time that it was better if I did not ask.

One day I was told to go to the tea dance at a certain hotel. I did not know that it was a well-known pick-up place, frequented by the better class of prostitutes. I was a very good dancer. My instructions were to dance with anyone who asked me and always to return to my own table. I was never to accept the offer to join someone at their table or to allow anyone to sit at my table, nor to accept a drink or anything else. Just to dance – and to ask questions. To find out the identity of my partners – not that they would necessarily tell me the truth, and to remember what they looked like.

After each afternoon Dr Marki asked me who I had been dancing with. Following several days of this routine, an Italian asked me to dance. He told me that he worked at the Italian Embassy and dealt with visa applications and that he only came on Wednesdays.

'Keep on going to the tea dance, as before,' said Dr Maki. 'If next Wednesday he is there and asks you to dance, invite him to sit at your table afterwards. Stay only for two more dances, which you dance with him and arrange to meet him the following Wednesday near the thermal baths on the Margaret Island.'

I did.

Whether or not he turned up the next Wednesday at the thermal baths I had no way of knowing, because by that time I had been caught and was being interrogated at the Police Station.

DR MARKI LIVED IN an elegant house. Its wide, open marble staircase led up to his offices on the first floor, the apartment where we lived was next door and there was a communicating door between the office and the apartment in the hallway.

One sunny afternoon at the beginning of June 1942, I was walking down the staircase. I was going to a tea dance. Halfway down the stairs I met two men coming up.

'Can you please tell us where is the office of Dr Marki?'

'On the first floor' I replied.

'Which door? Could you please show us?'

I did not think this peculiar; the house did not look like the location of a solicitor's office, even if there was a brass plate outside. So, brought up to be helpful, I went back up and rang the bell for them.

'Miss Iby, you forgot something? You forgot your key?' the maid asked.

'Oh, no, I only showed these gentlemen where the office was. They are here on business.'

'Have you an appointment?' the maid asked.

'No, but is Dr Marki in?'

'Yes, but he only sees people by appointment. Should I ask the clerk to make an appointment for you?'

I made to leave – not having any reason to wait, but one of the men caught my arm and pushed all three of us into the hallway, kicking the door shut behind them.

'We are from Security,' they said, flashing ID cards.

Pushing me in front of them they entered Dr Marki's office.

'You are both under arrest. You are coming with us. Nobody is to leave. We shall lock the place up. Whoever is in this place is to stay here. There will be a policeman outside. We shall decide who else is to come to the Police Station.'

'But why?' asked Dr Marki.

'We are not playing games. We are sure that you know why!'

I was too shaken to ask any questions. Dr Marki glanced at me – had I brought the Security Police to his place? I just shook my head and shuddered at the thought of what would happen now.

We were taken downstairs and bundled into a police car. There was no chance for us to talk – in any case I was too bewildered. When we arrived at the Police Station we were taken to separate rooms and the interrogation started.

The Woman Without A Number

They knew who I was and that I had entered Hungary illegally.

They knew I had an Aunt Bella and that I had stayed with Marton in his flat in Garay Street. I wondered, 'How did they find this out? Who had told them?' I knew very few people and hardly anybody knew me. Dr Marki had been taken with me, few people could talk to Gabriella and I was certain that neither she nor Father Andreas would have told. Marton was no longer in Budapest – that left only Aunt Bella. Would she have talked? If so, why?

There was other information they wanted from me: Who had come with me? How had I come from Bratislava? Who had helped me? Who had paid for it? Was I in touch with my father's officer friends? These were just for starters.

'I came on my own. I only met Aunt Bella and Marton, I have no idea who father's officer friends are. He never told me.'

'Who were you told to contact?'

'Only Father's sister, Aunt Bella. But I did not stay with her.'

They knew all about her, so this could not harm her. I wondered if she was being interrogated in another room. The questions went on and on – the interrogators changed from time to time but there was no let up and there was nothing I could tell them in reply to their accusations. It went on and on. After what seemed to me like hours, another officer came in and sent the one who had been interrogating me out of the room. He asked me whether I was hungry or thirsty.

'So thirsty,' I said.

He went to the door and asked for water to be brought. While we were waiting he offered me a cigarette. He lit it for me; there was a knock on the door. He went to the door, opened it and brought back a tray with a jug of water and two glasses. He poured out two glasses, picked one up and drank it. 'So that you know it's all right to drink,' he said. I did likewise, thirstily.

I remember that I had been told never to volunteer information, so I just sat and smoked my cigarette.

'When and where were you baptised?' he asked gently.

They had taken my handbag and would have found my baptismal certificate in it. I gave him the date on my baptismal certificate.

All of a sudden, the gentleness was gone. He slapped the table and shouted, 'Don't tell me lies. You could not have been baptised on that date; you were not in Hungary on that date. You are telling me lies. Not that it really matters – but you were never baptised, were you? This certificate is a forgery.' He tore it across. 'Who gave it to you?' I just shook my head.

'Who did it? When?' I stayed silent. Perhaps it would have been better not to admit that I had been baptised – but I still would have been asked who gave me the certificate.

'You will tell me eventually,' he said, 'it all depends on how hard you want your life to be.'

They came for me and put me in a small cell, with a concrete shelf for a bed. There was no window. The ceiling was high and a single bulb lit the place. The solid metal door clanked shut and the light went out – except for a sliver at the bottom of the door. I do not know how long I was there.

At intervals I was taken again to be interrogated – the questions were the same, started at the beginning and did not proceed any further than: 'Who gave you the certificate? Who else did you meet?

They had taken my bag, my watch, jewellery and shoes.

The intervals could have been minutes or hours; they seemed irregular. My cell was dark, but I must have been watched, because if I lay down and tried to close my eyes, a very bright light came on and a voice said, 'You must not sleep!'

The Woman Without A Number

Every so often a small hatch at the bottom of the door opened and bread and water were pushed in and the light stayed on for a few minutes but there was no discernable pattern in anything. I became completely disorientated, but was determined not to tell them that I had been meeting people on Dr Marki's orders and that I knew Father Andreas.

But in the end I did tell, after they used pliers to pull out the nail of the ring finger on my right hand – and I had been shown someone who had had his toenails pulled off and was a gibbering wreck.

Some time later I was taken again from my cell to see the 'nice' officer. He told me that I would be transferred to the women's prison in Ujpest in 'protective custody' while the examining magistrate investigated the whole matter. He also told me that we were bound to meet again, that we had unfinished business and I should not forget, that if it had not been for him, I would be in a much worse state.

The stunned, disorientated eighteen-year-old that was me, was put into a Black Maria and taken to the Ujpest women's prison.

PART TWO

4

*

Detained

Ionly have hazy memories of my arrival at the prison. Of being made to strip, to bath, my finger being roughly bandaged, eventually getting my clothes back, being taken along many passages and dumped in a large cell with bunk beds – except for two single beds. They indicated that one of them was for me, went out, and locked the door. There was one small window, high up. Windows started to become important to me.

I sat on the bed that had been allocated and looked at the two blankets. Not much later, the door was unlocked and a crowd of women came in. They gathered round me, asked me why I was there, what had I done.

I just shook my head, said I had done nothing, did not know why I was there. They hooted with laughter.

'You are one of us, none of us have done anything and none of us know why we are here,' they cackled.

In the course of time I found out that they had been sentenced for all sorts of things, from murder to shoplifting and soliciting.

The Woman Without A Number

The door was opened again and the wardress shouted at them to leave me alone, that I was in protective custody - in England this would be 'on remand' - and had not been sentenced, as they had been.

During the next week I learned from them a new language, the language of the street, the language of prison and from some of them, who were Gypsies, a few words of the Roma language.

I was the youngest there. When they realised that and that all I had really done was to illegally enter Hungary, the heckling and teasing stopped and they were actually quite kind to me.

Every morning they went to a workshop. As I was in protective custody I was not required nor allowed to work. After a few days, being locked up on my own with nothing to do, except for the weekly outing to the magistrate to be asked the same questions again and again, it became more than my mind could bear. I was allowed one book a week from the library but that lasted me just one day and the choice was extremely limited and not the type of book I usually read.

One day, when the wardress seemed less forbidding, I asked her whether there wasn't anything I could do to fill the time. I told her that I was good at sewing, that I had been trained by a dressmaker.

'Would you be willing to sew something for me?' she enquired.

'Of course,' I said, 'but I would need a sewing machine.'

The next day, after the other inmates had gone to the workshop, she opened the door and told me to go with her. I was taken to a small, bright single cell. On the table was a sewing machine.

'I have spoken to the Governor and, if you like to sew, we'll have quite a bit for you to do. But you know, this is quite unofficial, we can't pay you and what you are doing is voluntary.' I was only too glad to agree.

During the weeks I was in prison, I spent my days in that cell, making clothes. As I could not be paid, they brought me cakes, sweets, chocolates and cigarettes in return. I was told not to take anything back to the cell because the other inmates would want to know where the rewards came from, take them from me and make my life miserable. One was not supposed to be friendly with the guards. Nobody in the cell knew what I was doing. I was taken from there after they had gone to the workshop and came back before they returned.

I had been in prison for about a week when, at lunchtime, instead of the quite awful prison fare, a basket with food was brought to me. There was a flask of soup, a covered plate with meat and potatoes, salad, bread and fruit. I asked the wardress where it came from. She told me that prisoners in protective custody could have food sent in, if they could pay for it and that I must have arranged it myself. I had not; I had no money, I wondered whether, maybe, Aunt Bella's conscience had been pricked. But neither she, nor anyone else visited me during the three months I spent there, so I never found out. The food came from a nearby restaurant and I asked the wardress whether they could please ask the boy who brought the food, who had ordered it and was paying for it. All she knew or could find out was that it had been done by letter and that, every week, money was sent to them in an envelope. There was no name; there was nobody I could thank.

During one of the weekly interrogations by the examining magistrate I met Dr Marki coming from his interview. The two wardens decided to light a cigarette, which gave us an opportunity to have a few words. He told me, with tears in his eyes, that his daughter had contracted ptomaine poisoning while assisting in an autopsy and had died – and that they would not allow him to go to her funeral. He also told me that a total of 428 people had been arrested, that Father Andreas had been released on parole, and that all of us were only implicating each other. The examining magistrate was getting exasperated, things were getting more and more complicated, pressure was being put on him from many quarters; in all probability, the matter would be swept under the carpet. Too many important people were involved. I was told not to worry. It would all be all right.

In the examining magistrate's office I saw the piles of files become mountains; how the magistrate was becoming overwhelmed by the sheer quantity of paper. Corruption was rife in Hungary and I am certain that strings were being pulled. In the end it was decided not to take the case to court but to release all of us with just a warning.

When I was told I was to leave the prison I assumed I would go back either to Dr Marki, because I had nowhere else to go – or to Aunt Bella, if she would have me. I believed that they had decided not to proceed against me on all counts and that I could now stay in Hungary, legally. But I was mistaken.

On the sunny day I stepped out of the prison gate I was confronted by two men from the security police, who arrested me on a different charge, for the illegal entry into Hungary. They took me to the detention centre in Mosonyi Street.

ONLY MANY YEARS LATER, when I checked Dr Marki's witness statement, did I remember that I had ever been in the Mosonyi Street Detention Centre. The experience was so horrific that I buried the memory of it, although the scar on my jaw should have reminded me.

When the security police confronted me at the gates of the prison they told me that I was fortunate not to be sent back to Slovakia – and that was only because at present there was no extradition treaty between Slovakia and Hungary. They would take me to a place of safety until a decision was reached on what to do with me.

'Nothing can possibly be worse than being sent back,' they said.

A week later I wondered whether that was true.

The Detention Centre was the place where vagrants, beggars, drunks and prostitutes were held until the law dealt with them, as appropriate. There were huge dormitories with iron folding bedsteads which were stacked in one corner in the daytime. A long narrow table and benches went down the middle of the room, but there was not enough space for everyone to sit there. Those who had been there the longest had the choicest places nearest to the door. The ones who arrived last were put as far away as possible from there or had to sit on the stone floor against the walls.

In view of the lifestyle of the people who were incarcerated, on arrival everybody had to undergo a medical, which included a gynaecological examination – a new and highly unpleasant experience for me. I protested, but to no avail. It was the rule and nobody was exempt. It was understandable, as many of the inmates were prostitutes who would only be released if they had a clean bill of health or they were sent for treatment to the clinic for venereal diseases.

Every person got one blanket – usually the one used by the last person to leave. Hygiene was non-existent; there was one noisome toilet for the whole room of about thirty women and two cold-water taps. The bedsteads had a spring base on which you could spread the blanket so that the springs did not bite into you but then there was very little to cover yourself with and naturally – there were myriads of bedbugs at night.

After about a week, I had frightful itching sensations between my legs and a rash between my fingers as well as an itchy scalp. I had caught the lot – scabies, head lice and crab lice. I had no idea what was wrong with me, so I reported to the doctor, who enlightened me.

'You people bring these things in yourself – it's your way of life,' he said coldly.

I burst into tears. 'I don't understand what you mean. I have no idea what is causing this itch and I certainly had nothing wrong with me when I came in here.'

He had not really looked at me until then.

'Are you not on the streets?'

'Why should I be on the streets? I am a respectable girl. I am here because I came into Hungary illegally to escape from the Gestapo. I have already been kept in prison for three months for no reason whatsoever and when I was released without charge they brought me here. I do not know why I am here or what I have done to be brought to this ..... place.'

'You caught crab lice from the toilet and head lice from contact with the women. Scabies you must have caught in prison. It is very contagious, but takes at least two months to show itself. We can treat the crabs and the scabies. It's not pleasant but effective. Head lice? Everybody gets these. You get clean and within days they are back. As long as you are here, you won't be able to get rid of them for good. There is stuff for your head, but as there is not hot water to wash your hair...' He shrugged his shoulders.

'What do you do all day?' he asked.

'Nothing. There is nothing to do. I do not even understand what most of them are talking about.'

'I am not surprised,' said the doctor, 'you are among prostitutes and gypsies. What education do you have?'

I told him.

'Well, we can use some help here in the infirmary. Would you be willing to help? You could spend the day here but I am afraid that at night you would still have to be locked up with the others.'

I agreed wholeheartedly.

'But first we have to clear up these infections of yours.'

The process was neither pleasant nor painless but reasonably quick. I could not help in the infirmary until my hands were healed but after that I learned some basic skills; how to cut gauze into squares and make them into swabs, how to roll bandages, because they were used, washed, sterilised, re-rolled and re-used, how to bandage, dispense medicines, sterilise instruments, clean and dress wounds and even how to stitch them up – another way of using my handiness with the needle – and generally help the doctors. There were no nurses, only a couple of male orderlies.

I was a quick learner.

The doctor brought in some newspapers and the odd magazine and even, now and then, a medical journal. I asked to borrow them. I could read them in the infirmary but could not take them into the dormitory. When I had been at school, my aim had been to become a doctor – at least now I did something in that line of work.

My status in the dormitory changed dramatically. Whereas before, not being of the 'sisterhood', I was considered the lowest of the low, the last one to get food or a bedstead and often one with broken springs, now I was called 'the little doctor' and the women came to me with various problems, which they thought I could deal with quicker than if they had to queue up for the infirmary. In most cases they still had to come to the infirmary but often being able to talk helped. I also discovered that my hands frequently brought relief.

'My headache is much better since you put your hands on my head,' they'd say. 'You have the gift, you have healing hands,' added one old gipsy woman and she taught me how to read hands. This was knowledge with a mixed blessing, as I later found out.

I gradually gained confidence in this skill of healing – I closed my eyes, took a deep breath and concentrated, letting my hands go where they wanted to and do what they felt was required. It seemed to work and still does.

The nights in the dormitory were still purgatory; it was a noisy and foul place. Snoring, farting, mumblings, crying and swearing abounded, it was certainly not a place of rest.

One night, one of the women in the next dormitory started to scream and kept on doing so. All the lights came on, we all woke up and the warden went to investigate.

The screaming woman was complaining of awful pains in her side. 'There is no doctor here during the night. You just have to put up with it,' she snapped. 'Get the little doctor, get her to come,' said one of the women. 'She'll help.' We were not supposed to leave our dormitory after lights out nor enter into another one. We were all awake by now and the warden called me from the doorway. I went with her to the screaming woman, who was twisting around and sweating profusely.

Whatever could I do? I was no doctor – there was obviously something seriously wrong with her and she was in evident pain.

'Can you get the doctor?' I asked the warden.

'You know quite well that no doctor would come out during the night,' she responded tersely.

'Can you send her to a hospital?'

'I can't do that without the doctor's instructions.'

'What can I do?' I said.

'I don't know, but they asked for you. I know I shouldn't do it – but stay with her for a bit, maybe she'll calm down.'

'I'll need a light.'

'Sorry, but I have to put the lights out before the whole place goes berserk.' said the warden, 'and I cannot let you have my torch, they would brain you with it if they got violent. On second thoughts – maybe you should go back to your bed.'

But the woman's neighbours started to wail and promised to see that I was safe.

'Do you think you'll be safe?' asked the warden dubiously.

I assured her that I doubted the women were going to attack me, since they had asked for me. So I sat on the side of the woman's bed, talked to her and stroked her head and her side. It seemed that the pain gradually subsided – it was probably just colic – and after a while I went to the door and knocked to be let out. The warden let me out and took me to my dormitory.

'I can't put the light on again, it will wake them all up. You'll just have to find your own bed in the dark.'

I did not think I would have a problem, all I had to do was count the shadows. I started to number the cots along the left wall, I thought that mine was the fourteenth. When I came to it and started to lower myself on to it I realised that I must have miscounted – there was somebody in it. I grasped the iron edge and turned my head away so as not to fall on the sleeper. If anyone got woken up suddenly they were liable to become violent and falling on someone would have been interpreted as an attack.

Some time in my childhood, I had broken my left wrist and it was not strong enough to support me as I turned my head, so that my jaw hit the edge of the cot. I felt the impact and something sticky but thought no more about it. I was tired, so I crawled on to the next cot and fell asleep.

The next morning I was shaken awake amid shouts. The upper part of the cot and my face and hands were covered in blood. I had a frightful pain on the left side of my jaw. There was no mirror anywhere so I had no idea what was wrong.

The women were shouting and hammering on the door.

'The little doctor has been attacked. She is covered in blood.'

I reassured them that I had not been attacked. I would have been aware of something like that; nevertheless, I could not imagine how I had become injured. Then I remembered.

I was taken to the infirmary. When the blood had been washed away it was seen that there was a gash on my jaw and that it needed a few stitches. I had a stiff jaw for some time; the wound healed cleanly, but I have the scar of it to this day.

I must have been in Mosonyi Street Detention Centre several weeks – and was even getting used to it, in a way. You can get used to anything, eventually, particularly if you do not know whether it is ever going to end or what is going to happen next. Then, one day, I was told that I was to be moved to the refugee camp in Szabolcs Street.

I DO NOT KNOW what the original purpose of the building was which housed the camp for Jewish refugees from Austria and Slovakia in Szabolcs Street. Like most houses in Budapest it had been built as a hollow square, but as far as I remember it was a single storey building. Once through the heavy double gates, the guards' quarters and the offices were on the left. Next to them were the men's dormitories and, across the square, the women's ones. All dormitories had two-tiered bunk beds. On the left side were the day rooms, where the men played cards and chess and the dining rooms. On the right was the washhouse with separate ablution facilities for men and women. I think that there must have also been a day room for women but, since I spent most of my time watching the men playing chess or wandering around the central paved area, I can't remember that.

I knew nobody and nobody knew me. Most of the people were in family groups or had already formed friendships. I was a latecomer, made to feel an intruder.

Money was a problem; I had none. I exchanged my two gold pieces. Whether I got a fair rate of exchange I had no way of knowing but I needed money for cigarettes. If you did not smoke or were unable to offer a cigarette you were an outcast.

It did not take long for my small supply of money to run out. Now, I would not accept a cigarette if I were in a group of women smokers because the few I had left would have been gone in one round when it was my turn to offer a return smoke. If I was watching the men play chess I never took out my cigarettes. There was enough smoke around to inhale nicotine second-hand. Now and then, one of the men would insist that I had one of their cigarettes but most of them either smoked cigars or a pipe – cigarettes were not really considered to be manly. Eventually those were the only smokes I had. I think I must have got money from Aunt Bella from time to time, but it was never very much and never lasted long.

There were some excellent musicians amongst the men and, whatever else they had left behind, they had brought their instruments with them. Many evenings became concerts or impromptu jam sessions. There was no piano, so it was mainly violins, violas, flutes, clarinets, saxophones, oboes, a couple of cellos and even – miraculously – a double bass. Percussion instruments were improvised with spoons, chairs, tables, pots or anything else which could produce an appropriate sound. It was nearly as if the Viennese Symphony Orchestra had been there – and perhaps it was.

The guards were security men and there was a changeover every week. We women kept out of their way, as far as possible.

I had been at the camp for some weeks when, after a particular guard change I was accosted by one of the officers as I was crossing the square.

'Remember me? 'He asked. I recognised him. It was the 'nice' man who had interrogated me months ago at the police station. 'I told you we would meet again.'

'So we have,' I replied.

'I was kind to you, wasn't I?' He asked.

I nodded. Kind had been a comparative virtue.

'You owe me. I'll see you tonight,' he said.

I was somewhat puzzled. Lights out was at ten, by which time we all had to be in our bunks. I thought no more about it, went to bed as usual, in my top bunk.

The guards used to patrol the dormitories with torches during the night, ostensibly to ensure that everybody was where they were supposed to be, that a wife had not sneaked across to meet her husband or vice versa. Cards with our names on were fixed with drawing pins to the sides of our beds. I was fast asleep when I was shaken awake. It was one of the guards.

'The officer wants you, get dressed, come along.'

In the bottom bunk was Clara, a German refugee, who had been there some time. In German she said softly, 'You do not have to go. He cannot force you to go.'

'He thinks I owe him,' I whispered back.

'You only owe to yourself. If you go with him, the others will also ask for you – and do you want that? Once you have agreed to be with one ...'

I turned to the guard, 'Tell him, I'm sorry, but it's the wrong time.'

'Does that matter?' he asked

'It does to me.'

He shrugged and left.

The next morning I was stopped by the guard officer.

'You did not come!' he said.

'I told the guard why.'

'Will you come tonight?'

'Sorry, but no,' I replied.

'Not tonight and not any night?'

I hesitated, he had put me on the spot. I remembered what Clara had said.

I shook my head.

'It's your loss,' he said, 'others will.' And he walked off.

To be in Budapest, even in a refugee camp, was considered a privilege. You were near to the fleshpots, could have visitors and even stood a chance of release, if you could find a sponsor. And people with enough money could bribe their way out now and then for a short period of freedom, although never an entire family, one person had to stay behind as hostage. And there were other ways of gaining privileges.

As far as I was concerned, I was penniless and evidently had just forfeited my chance of privileges. It did not, therefore, really surprise me when two days later, I was transported to the refugee camp in Ricse, a god-forsaken place as far away from Budapest as it was possible to go.

The warm fug of Szabolcs Street was exchanged for a cold, grim, windswept hillside.

5

*

Close To Ella

I have no memory of the journey itself but, once there, the camp was large and built on a piece of sloping ground.

It consisted of brick single storey buildings, each of four rooms with a toilet and washroom. In each room on two sides were wooden, slatted platforms on which mattresses were placed. There was a narrow gangway between the two rows of mattresses. There was also a small iron stove. In really cold weather - and by now it was late autumn - we got an allocation of a small bucket of coal to stop us from freezing. As far as I can recall, there were eight women in each room.

There was a camp for the men as well but, except on rare occasions, there was little communication between the two and I cannot recall anything about the men's camp.

There was one block comprising the kitchen and dining room and, a short distance away, some workshops which included, fortunately for me, a sewing room.

On arrival I was given a sack, directed to a barn and told to fill the sack with straw – it was to be my bed.

The sewing workshop proved to be my salvation, as by sewing I could earn money or be paid in cigarettes. Also, it was heated in the daytime. There was a small shop, open for a few hours each day where we could buy cigarettes, sweets, writing paper, stamps and tea.

Prior to my arrival, the carpentry workshop where the supporting platforms for the mattresses were built, had supplied us with wood off-cuts to light our fires. When it got too cold we even used a few of the slats to light the fire. Here one had to be careful; too many slats gone and mattresses ended up on the floor. The result: an investigation by camp staff and some sort of penalty.

The workshop had also built a stage in the dining hall and the sewing room had made stage curtains. There were many talented singers, actresses and dancers among the inmates and once a month a show was given. The officers, guards and their families came, seated in the front rows.

My own talents were far too paltry to compete with these professional artists, as shown by an unsuccessful audition, so I helped with the scenery and props. The group of entertainers spent most of their time rehearsing – and, provided that you did not comment or giggle, you could attend.

The food was dismal; the main staple was maize porridge – now fashionable as polenta. I have been unable to face it ever since – even in a fashionable restaurant.

All able-bodied men in the village of Ricse had gone into the army and there was a severe shortage of agricultural labour. If you volunteered to work on the land, you could go out of the camp, albeit accompanied by guards, and the villagers on whose land you worked shared their midday meal with you. It was just home-baked bread, butter, perhaps a little cheese or a slice of salami or half an onion – and lots of milk. Under the circumstances I even drank the milk, although I had always hated it.

The Woman Without A Number

The first task we were set to was the removal of tares from the cereal crop. Later on, we helped with hay making and then with the harvest. The old men and some of the guards cut the crop; we tied the sheaves and carried them to the threshing machine where they were heaved up into the thresher. The stalks had then to be gathered up again, made into sheaves and stacked. It was prickly, hot and tiring work, but we were fed and those of us who could speak Hungarian talked, sang and jested with the village women.

One other way to escape the monotony of the camp was to go to church on Sunday morning. There were quite a few of us who had been baptised and the walk to and from church, although accompanied by guards, was pleasant. The service, catholic and in Latin, did not have much meaning for me. Some of the people from the camp took communion – I abstained and stayed in my pew.

We were allowed to receive mail and to send out one letter per week. Ingoing and outgoing letters were censored. The camp office considered all this an additional thankless task, so the length of a letter was restricted to a single page. We practised writing smaller and smaller to get as much as possible on to one page but this was counterproductive, because if the officer could not read the letter, he tore it up. This restriction on communication was hard to bear for many, especially for mothers who had been interned but whose children, being minors, had been allowed to stay with relatives or friends.

Our liberty was severely restricted, particularly once the harvest had been gathered in and there was no more need for extra field hands. Potatoes and root crops were gathered in by the children who, traditionally, got special school holidays for this purpose.

Our biggest misery were the bedbugs which infested all buildings, not only in the camp but, as I had experienced, practically every inhabited building in Hungary. When I had stayed with Marton and Dr Marki one ensured that the legs of the beds were placed in tins filled with liquid - I think it was creosote - which created a barrier to bedbugs. You had to make certain that no part of the bed or the bedclothes touched the walls as that was where the bugs were.

We were driven frantic by these pests. We reasoned – not being native Hungarians and unaware of the habitat of these blood suckers – that if we chipped off all the plaster, washed the wall with a pesticide we would get rid of them. It took us days and days and we despatched colony after colony of bedbugs to their death. We put up with the mess, the dust, the broken fingernails and the hoots of derision from the native Hungarians, including the guards. We were determined that we were going to have a bug-free environment and undisturbed nights.

Finally we were down to the bare brick. We saturated the walls with pesticide, choking in the fumes we scrubbed down the wooden platforms that were our beds with the same liquid, got new sacks and fresh straw. We washed our blankets, dried them in the sun and were ready to have our first un-bitten night in our smelly room.

We only had candles for lights. We put them out and, as it was a warm night, opened the window which was above my bed, and settled down. We woke about half an hour later shrieking and lit our candles. The blankets were crawling with bedbugs. They lived in the brickwork itself and the plaster which we had so laboriously removed had actually prevented all of them getting at us.

I picked up my blanket, stood up on the bed and shook it out of the window. Howls from outside greeted this action. The guards were standing near to the window, watching our performance and they received a rain of bedbugs as a reward for their voyeurism. All our work had not only been in vain, we had actually worsened the situation. The only way to get rid of bedbugs is to burn them – preferably together with the building that houses them.

We were at a loss what to do but some men came over and concreted our wall, which now sweated in the winter but the bedbugs were fewer – for a time at least. Any we caught we threw into the fire or even into the flame of a candle. They really do stink when burning, I shall never forget the horrible stench.

I had been in Ricse a few months when I heard that my family, that is mother, father, grandmother, my brother Tomy and my cousin Magda had arrived in Budapest and that Mother and Father were in an internment camp with my brother, while my grandmother, due to her age, had been allowed to stay temporarily with Aunt Bella and Magda with cousins of her father. Tomy and Magda were about thirteen years old at the time.

More than once it crossed my mind that if I had acceded to the request of the security officer I would now be with my parents in Budapest, yet it was no use thinking of what might have been.

It was possible to obtain temporary leave on compassionate grounds from Ricse. I applied, explaining that it had been a long time since I had seen my family and got three days' absence. Since it took the best part of a day to travel by train from Ricse to Budapest, this was not overgenerous; however the office provided me with a travel warrant.

When I arrived in Budapest I made my way to Aunt Bella, where I met Grandmother, whose beautiful auburn hair had turned completely white. She told me of their adventures during their escape from Slovakia, that my grandfather had died and that Aunt Janka and Uncle George were in a camp in Slovakia.

It was during this stay that I met Gaspar. We liked each

other instantly. Gaspar was actually his family name - his first name was Janos - but that was such a common name that everybody, including me, called him Gaspar. He was tall, dark haired, very attractive, generous and probably about thirty years old when we met. What struck me most was that he was very kind and at that time, and even now, kindness was the quality I esteemed most.

After I returned to Ricse he sent me funny little notes attached to packets of cigarettes. They made the guards in the office laugh – and I got my cigarettes.

My parents applied for permission for me to join them for Christmas, and I, along with many others, was permitted to do so. It made sense, since it allowed most of the guards to be also with their families. I was fortunate in being given a week. During this time Gaspar and I got to know each other well. He asked me to marry him and, with my parents' agreement, we became engaged. Gaspar was in the film industry; he was considered essential to the war effort and did not think that he would be called up.

There was no reason for us to wait. We planned to get married in June and Gaspar started the necessary official procedures and applications to get me released from the internment camp.

Life seemed to be looking up. Gaspar pulled strings and after a couple of months I was called to the office and told that I would be released on parole, but not, to my disappointment, to Budapest. Did I have family elsewhere in Hungary? I wrote to father and he replied that his uncle ran a printing house in Szekesfehervar, not far from Lake Balaton, and I was to stay there until my wedding in June, when I could move to Budapest to live with Gaspar. I would then no longer be considered a refugee but a resident and would be able to petition the release of my parents and brother on parole.

The Woman Without A Number

The date of my parole release approached. We were still very restricted on correspondence and used all possible means to smuggle mail out, not least because one felt restricted in what one wrote, knowing that everything would be read in the office and become common knowledge among the guards.

Some of my friends asked whether I would take a letter out for them. It was considered too dangerous an action if one only had a weekend pass, because as a punishment it could be withdrawn, but I was going out on permanent parole. I would have to report to the police at Szekesfehervar on arrival, on a date given and the office at Ricse would be powerless to cancel it. I was due to leave on a Friday morning. Against my better judgment I accepted letters from others and put them inside my suspender belt. These were quite wide and substantial affairs in those days even if you were slim. I packed my bag, said my goodbyes and reported to the office for my travel warrant and the papers that I had to present to the police at Szekesfehervar.

'Are you ready to go?' asked the guard commandant.

'Of course,' I replied.

'And what are you taking with you?'

'This bag and my handbag' I said.

'Open them up.'

I did. They searched the contents carefully.

'And where are the letters you are taking out?'

'What letters?'

'Don't play the innocent with me. I know that you are taking out letters for some people.'

I protested. Who had shopped me? There had to be a limit to how many letters I could conceal about my person, so I had asked my friends not to tell anybody that I was taking out letters for them. Officially I said no to everybody. Who could have been so mean? What possible advantage could anyone have for betraying my friends and me?

A female guard was called. I was strip-searched and naturally, the letters were found.

My subsequent interview with the Commandant was highly unpleasant. To say that he wiped the floor with me is putting it mildly. 'Why?' he kept on asking 'Why was I so stupid to jeopardise my release? Was this a worthwhile action when freedom was offered to me?'

To tell the truth, I had not considered that I was doing anything monumentally wrong. I had felt that out of loyalty to the women with whom I had shared a room, food, smokes, laughter and tears for months this was the least I could do. I knew that others had done it before and had not been caught. Yes, we were restricted on mail; yes, everything that went in and out of the camp was censored, but surely no letter could possibly contain a state secret or anything of momentous importance to anyone except the sender and the recipients who were, anyway, family members. I never said any of this, I did not get the chance to do so nor would it have made any difference. I, who had never transgressed the rules, who had been amiable and on friendly terms with the guards, had let him down, had done wrong and would have to be punished. I was marched to the punishment block.

My friends who had gathered near the gate to wave me off saw me, instead, being led in the opposite direction.

A little while later those of my friends who had given me letters to take out were collected, taken to the Commandant's office and then also marched to the punishment block.

I was put into a small, windowless room with a heap of straw in one corner. The door was locked on me. I heard the others being put into cells as well, but in twos. Probably, there were not enough cells for everyone to suffer solitary confinement.

The walls were too thick for us to communicate by knocking and when one of them called out, she was told that talking was forbidden and that each time a voice was heard the period of detention would be extended by an hour. I had not been told how long mine would be.

Being locked up on my own, in the dark, brought back all the horrors of the time I had spent in the cell at the police station.

After some time – probably hours – the cell door was opened, a jug of water, a piece of bread and a tin bucket were put in and the door locked again. Crawling along the floor I found the bread and water, ate and drank. Some time later I heard the doors being unlocked and steps on the stone floor, my friends were being released. It must have been Friday night. My watch had been taken, not that it would have helped, as it was completely dark. I had no idea of the passage of time. I made myself as comfortable as possible on the prickly straw and eventually slept in fits and starts.

It was probably morning when another piece of bread and another jug of water were brought in and the bucket changed. This happened five times. In between I crouched on the straw and shivered.

On the next occasion that the door was opened I was told to come out. A light was burning; it was either dawn or dusk. Shaking and unsteady on my feet I was marched to the Commandant's office.

'I would like to have kept you locked up for many more days on bread and water but you have to report to the police at Szekesfehervar today. Had you not been so foolish you could have spent the weekend with your family and friends in Budapest. It is now Monday morning. You will be escorted to shower and change and then taken to the station to catch the first train to Budapest, where you have to change trains. You should just make it to the police station in Szekesfehervar before they close up in the evening. I hope that I won't see you here again.'

I did as I was told, had just time between changing trains in Budapest to ring Gaspar and to tell him what had happened. I asked him to ring Uncle Eisler in Szekesfehervar and let him know that I would arrive that evening.

UNCLE EISLER WAS AT the station to meet me and came with me to the police station. There I was told that I had to report once a week, on Thursday mornings, and was asked for the address where I would be staying. Uncle Eisler, father's uncle, explained that I would be staying with his married daughter who had a little girl, as I would be her governess. He took me to their apartment and introduced me. I call her Ella, but that was not her real name. However hard I try, I cannot remember it.

She was a buxom, lively, blonde woman on her second marriage. Jeno, her fifteen-year-old son from her first lived with her and her husband, Ferenc. They had a five-year-old daughter, Gaby. Ferenc doted on Ella and adored the little girl. He was a jeweller and Ella a dressmaker, employing four girls. I was to look after Gaby and cook the midday meal for the family.

I had learned some cooking from my grandmother, but my repertoire was strictly limited and I had little experience. I can still remember the ghastly occasion when Ferenc brought some live carp for dinner. Fish were usually bought live because that was the only way to ensure that they were really fresh. They arrived covered in damp newspaper and were dumped on the kitchen table. I unwrapped them and they started to flop about, I had no idea what to do with them.

Ferenc said, 'You have to kill them first.'

'How?' I replied, somewhat aghast.

The Woman Without A Number

'You bang them on the back of the head.'

I banged away, they flopped away.

The banging brought Gaby into the kitchen.

'What are you doing, Iby?' the little girl asked.

'I am trying to kill the fish.'

'Mummy, mummy, Iby is killing the fish,' she shouted.

'I am trying to kill them, but they won't die, they keep on flopping about.'

Ella joined us and then Ferenc.

No banging on the head would stop the poor fish from flopping about.

'They have to be killed before they are cooked,' said Ella, stating the obvious.

'I am not going to eat them. Don't kill them. Put them in the bath. I'll take them back to the river later,' said Gaby.

'Nonsense,' said Ferenc, 'they are today's dinner. Give me the knife, this is what you have to do!'

Picking up the big kitchen knife Ferenc proceeded to saw off the head of the fish, which continued to flop about even without their head on.

Gaby and Ella ran screaming from the kitchen.

I would have liked to do the same but knew that I had to cook dinner, come what may. Eventually Ferenc managed to cut off the heads of all the fish and I was left to gut and scale them. Gutting was simple, Grandmother had shown me how to do that but it was a tricky business getting their scales off when there was no head and no gills to hook your fingers into.

Eventually the fish were more or less scale-less, filleted and fried and we had a rather late dinner; all of us, except for Gaby, who would not touch the fish nor eat any fish thereafter. I couldn't really blame her; after that I didn't have much liking for fish either.

Gaspar sent me money and loving letters. I bought fabric

and Ella helped me to make my trousseau. I bought the wedding rings from Ferenc. Letters travelled between my parents in Budapest and me and we were all looking forward to my coming to Budapest after the wedding at the beginning of June.

Ferenc and Ella had a summerhouse at Balatonfured on Lake Balaton. It was locked up during the winter. On the weekend before Easter, Ferenc, Jeno and I took the local train there, armed with cleaning materials and bed linen to air and clean the place and to make it ready for our stay there over the forthcoming holiday period. Coming back, the train was full of rumours that the Germans had occupied Hungary. We could not credit it; after all, Hungary was Germany's ally, its army was fighting alongside the Germans on the Eastern Front, so why would Hungary be occupied? But the sad thing was – it was true. Being an ally of Germany did not make a country immune from occupation.

The first thing the German army did was to take all the cattle and grain from the farms and stores. All the geese also seemed to have disappeared, as had the chickens and there were no more eggs to be had on the market. Next, new laws were introduced. All Hungarian Jews had to wear the yellow star – not being Hungarian that did not apply to me – and had to obey a curfew.

This created an awkward situation in our household. Ella's first husband had been a Catholic and she had been baptised. Jeno had been Catholic from birth; so neither Ella, Jeno nor I had to wear the yellow star but Ferenc, Gaby and Uncle and Aunt Eisler did.

A curfew had been a condition of my parole but applied only after ten o'clock. Ferenc, Gaby and the Eislers had to be at home by eight, Ella and Jeno could stay out all night.

Most of Ella's customers were Jewish. Their interest in

71

new clothes vanished; trade dropped off and the girls in the workshop were dismissed. Ferenc, afraid of his shop being looted, closed it down. The Germans took over the Eisler printing house. Money was getting scarce. It was suggested that I should find a position as a governess with another family, a non-Jewish one by preference – never mind that a condition of my parole was that I should live with Ella's family, that problem could probably be fixed.

The local paper had many advertisements for governesses. I had good qualifications, I spoke German, French and English, played the piano, was well read, could knit, crochet, embroider and sew. I applied for two posts and was interviewed in both cases and offered the job but when I explained my circumstances - that I was a refugee and had to report each week to the police - the offer was withdrawn and I was advised to seek employment with a Jewish family. So I had to stay put.

Gaspar continued to send me money and I now paid Ella for my keep but it was not an easy situation. I had been foisted on them and they would now have preferred it if I was somewhere else. I assured them and myself, that this unwelcome stay would not last long, that within a couple of weeks I would be married, off their hands and in Budapest.

One morning I had taken Gaby to see her grandparents and we had just left their house when we were stopped by a German patrol.

'Why are you not wearing the yellow star?' they barked at me in German. I had no idea why they assumed that everyone would understand the language. In impeccable German I replied: 'I don't have to wear it.'

'But your child wears the star.'

'This is not my child. I am her governess.'

I bent down to Gaby and told her, in Hungarian, to run quickly back to her Grandma.

'What did you tell the child?'

'I told her to go back home. We were going for a walk.'

'You speak good German. Are you German?' they asked.

'No,' I replied, 'Austrian.'

'That's the same, don't you know that? What are you doing here? Why are you not working in Germany? Show me your papers,' they demanded.

I searched my pockets. Somehow – fortuitously – I had left the identity card which had been issued to me by the police, at Ella's.

'Sorry, I did not bring them with me.'

'Don't you know that it is the law to carry your identity card with you at all times. You had better come with us.'

I was taken to the local Gestapo headquarters. It was an occasion when telling the truth would have had fatal consequences. I borrowed the identity of my brother's last nanny, Fraulein Trude. I remembered enough about her to give a convincing report about myself/her, of my/her brother who was a protestant priest, which did not impress them.

Why had I not returned to Germany to help the war effort, as all self-respecting Germans abroad had been urged to do? How could I demean myself by working as a Governess for a Jewish family?

I told them that only the father was Jewish, that I was engaged to be married to a Hungarian, both of which statements, albeit true, were greeted with derision. I promised to better myself, to break off my engagement, to return to Germany and to do my duty – and was allowed to leave.

I had had a serious fright and, had I had my ID card with me, I would not have been freed.

I told Ella and Ferenc that I had been stopped and interrogated. We agreed that walking in the centre of the town was now dangerous. Ferenc was abnormally anxious about Gaby, who was their second child. Their first, also a girl, had died of meningitis before she was six years old and he had a premonition that Gaby would not reach her sixth birthday either.

'If she dies, I'll kill myself,' he said more than once.

It was now May 1944.

There were frequent air raid warnings and anti aircraft fire and the thump of the occasional bomb could be heard.

On the first Thursday morning at the beginning of June I went to the police station and reported, as normal – always to the same officer. After a few weeks he had asked me to go out with him. I explained that I was engaged to be married – which he did not consider a barrier to going out, but one that I did. Each Thursday there was friendly banter between us but he did not ask me out again, except on this occasion when he asked me to have a meal with him in the evening and to spend the night with him. He was very insistent. 'It'll be worth your while,' he said several times. But I was steadfast and refused. I often wondered what my life would have been like had I accepted.

Later that evening there were air raids again. Jeno phoned from a friend's house and told us he would spend the night there. We went to bed as usual, it was the 5th June 1944.

PART THREE

6

*

To Auschwitz

It was a particularly balmy night and I had opened the windows wide in the living room where I slept on a folding bed. The 'All Clear' had not yet gone when I went to bed. In a few days I would be married.

It was dawn when I heard heavy feet tramping up the stairs and loud knocks on the door.

'You have ten minutes to get your things – you are all coming with us. Take food,' said the voices on the other side.

Ella and Ferenc packed jewellery, valuables and food, took money from the hidden safe. I packed some clothes for Gaby.

I had told the soldiers that this could not apply to me, that I would not go, as I was not a Hungarian Jew. 'You'll have a chance to explain this; we have been told to take everybody who lives here,' they said.

'Where are you taking us?' I asked.

'To the brickyard.'

I was certain that I would be able to talk my way out of this situation, so I took only my handbag with the wedding rings I had bought, the heavy gold necklace and bracelet Gaspar had bought me – and my papers. There was a lot of corruption about – I thought I might be able to buy my freedom with the gold. I took no food, no blankets, and no clothes.

That day – or the next – we heard that the Invasion had started, so we were certain that whatever lay before us could not last long, because we imagined that the Americans or the British would be with us within weeks, if not days.

At the entrance to the brickyard we were registered; they took all our money, jewellery and valuables. The officer to whom I had to report at the police station on Thursdays was there. I got into the line that he was dealing with. Surely he knew that I should not have been brought here. When I got to him, I took my papers out and told him; 'I should not have been brought here. I do not come under the Jewish Laws; I should not be detained. You know that I am registered with the police. Please, please tell them that I should not be here.'

'I'm sorry,' he said, 'it's too late now. There is nothing I can do. You were with the Jews, so you have to go with them. You know, you did not have to be with them, you could have been somewhere else.'

He took the rings, the necklace and bracelet, the little money I had and my ID card. He gave me a receipt. There was now no way for me to prove who I was. All I had was a slip of paper, saying: two rings, a bracelet, a necklace of yellow metal, an ID card.

What I did not know at the time, and did not discover until sixty years later, was that he had entered me on the list as a 'political prisoner', not as a Jew, which might have made a difference to my fate.

Ella, Ferenc and Gaby met up with the Eislers and set up a family enclave in a corner of the brickyard. I felt like an intruder. They took stock of what food they had brought with them. It became evident that one extra mouth would reduce the length of time their provisions would last. Nobody knew how long we would be held there or what would become of us.

At midday a kind of soup was brought into the campsite and I went to get some. Most people took some – their own provisions would last that much longer if they took what was offered. In the evening, people's own provisions had to provide a meal. Old Ma Eisler offered me a piece of bread and a couple of slices of salami. I took them gratefully, but decided that I would not become a burden to them any longer. After all, until a few months before, they had not even known of my existence.

Next morning I went to explore the brickyard. Spare bricks had been used to raise the walls around one area. All Jewish patients had been decanted from the local hospital; some who had just been operated on, women who had just given birth, chronically sick people, some with TB as well as people from mental institutions who had been sectioned. Patients lay on straw in two lines and doctors, in their traditional white coats, administered to them. I approached one of them:

'Can I help you?' I asked.

'Are you a nurse?'

'No, but I did help the doctor in the infirmary at the detention centre in Budapest.'

'We are grateful for any help,' he said. 'We have no nurses here, they have all joined their families and who can blame them? But the Hippocratic Oath requires medical people to help the sick, whatever happens. Bring your things over and join us.'

'I have nothing to bring. I am not supposed to be here but nobody will listen to me.'

The Woman Without A Number

'You are needed here,' he said.

We were an odd assortment of doctors, dentists, vets and helpers, the latter with very limited knowledge, just like me.

There was little sleep for us during the next nights. We took drugs - I think it was Ephedrine - to stay awake. I dressed wounds, bandaged, soothed and calmed. The doctors had brought their medical kit with them and also what medicaments they had in their surgeries. Those who had been on duty at the hospital had also taken as much as they could of the contents of the pharmaceutical department. After a couple of days, some of the women with newborn babies were claimed by their families but nobody asked for the very seriously ill or the mentally deranged.

The day of my proposed wedding came and went.

I wondered whether Gaspar knew what had happened to me, whether he had, all unknowing, come to Szekesfehervar when I did not turn up in Budapest and found me gone, whether he had made any efforts to find me, to get me released. Each morning I went to the guards' office and asked whether anyone had come looking for me. Every day the answer was the same, 'Nobody is allowed in or out.'

After four or five days, the senior doctor called us together.

'I now know what is going to happen. We are all going to be transported by train to a concentration camp. I do not think that people who are ill or old or weak will survive. It might be even too hard for those of us who are fit and able. You may prefer to end matters yourself rather than put up with torture and degradation. Everybody has a breaking point. I have some tablets here. Each of you may have one of these. If things get too bad, it will give you a quick way out. I do hope that you will not need to use them.'

Along with everybody else I accepted a tablet from him. I kept mine right to the end of the nightmare.

The same evening we were told we would be moved the following day. The senior doctor offered us sleeping pills; he thought that after the drugs we had been taking to keep awake it was unlikely we would rest otherwise and sleep was certainly needed to give us strength for what was to follow.

I slept that night deeply and dreamlessly. We were woken at dawn. On the railway line next to the brickyard a train of cattle wagons arrived with some straw in each. Gradually the campsite emptied as the wagons were filled with people herded like sheep who did not even bleat. There was no weeping, no resistance. Whatever made us so compliant?

We found a married elderly couple, both of them doctors, had taken their pills and were dead. We lifted them on two stretchers and laid them side-by-side in the entrance of the hospital for all to see and to say their farewell to them, for they had been well liked in the community.

When we left – we were the last ones – they were still there, looking just like sculptures on a heraldic tomb. I do hope they were given a decent burial.

There were two wagons for the patients, with at least one doctor and helper in each. Fortunately there was a little more space in these wagons. We laid the patients on the straw; there was a bucket in one corner and the doctors and helpers made one corner their own. The door was slid shut. Only a small slit of a window high up let in light. The train moved off. There were stops now and then but we had no idea where we were going. On one occasion when we stopped, there was a passenger train on a parallel line, which was also waiting. I think there was an air raid in progress. We must have been in Poland by then. I asked to be lifted up and looked out of the window. Women in headscarves in the other train were pointing at us, crossing themselves and holding up their hands as in prayer. Some were weeping.

That night a dentist in our group crawled over to me.

'Hold me,' he whispered, putting his arms around me, 'This might be the last time I can touch a human being.' We didn't even know each other's names, but held each other close for a long time.

I can't remember how long the journey lasted, probably two or three days. When the train finally stopped and the doors were slid open we saw some very thin men in striped pyjamas with shaved heads.

'Leave all your things here,' someone said. 'Leave all sick people here. Leave all small children and old people here. Only those who are fit are to get out. Men this side, women that side. Make up lines of five. Hurry, hurry, hurry.'

Our five were two women doctors, a dentist, a nurse and I and we tried to stay together from that day onwards.

We watched as the people in front of us were marched forward, some selected to go to the right, some to the left. We five had been working together for some days. We looked at each other.

'We stay together,' I said, 'let's link arms and go forward together laughing. Put a scarf over your head,' I told the dentist whose hair was prematurely grey. She did.

Dr Mengele, who was doing the selection, saw us coming, stepping out together, laughing, laughed himself, made a remark to a woman beside him and waved us to the right through a gate over which the inscription read 'ARBEIT MACHT FREI' - work makes you free. We had arrived in Oswieczin, later known as Auschwitz-Birkenau.

THOSE OF US WHO had been sent through the gates were re-formed into fives and marched towards some huts. We were crammed into a room and told to strip but to keep our shoes with us. In fives we were then told to go into another room and to sit on low stools. A man in striped pyjamas stood behind each stool armed with barber's clippers. In front of us stood uniformed armed Germans of both sexes.

They shaved first of all the hair on our heads, then our armpits and between our legs. The German guards found it very amusing. We were told next to remove earrings and any other jewellery we might have. Since the Hungarian had taken all I had, all they got from me were my gold ear studs that had been hidden by my hair. There was not much to collect from any of us and the Germans were not particularly pleased about that.

We were told to open our mouth and another man in striped pyjamas came with pliers to remove any gold teeth. We were then told to go into the next room, where we had to give our personal details – name, place and date of birth, occupation and nationality. All this was entered in a book. Each of us was given a number. For reasons unknown to me we were one of the few transports not to have the number tattooed on our left arm. I could not remember mine and have nothing to remind me of it but have recently found out that it was 25.245.

Then we were pushed into another room and told to drop our shoes. When the room was crammed full, a door at the opposite side opened into a large, concrete space with showers in the ceiling. We were pushed in under the cold showers. No soap, no towels, naturally. Then into another room to find our shoes and where we were given some garments to wear. They were stiff and smelled strongly of disinfectant, a smell that we got used to during the time we spent in Auschwitz.

Back into fives and a column of us was marched off, along a dusty road along which we saw wired enclosures on each side with hutments inside – like large cages for dangerous animals. We entered one enclosure. We had arrived at our destination.

The long hut had one separate room at the entrance, on the right, for the Capos, who were in charge of each hut. The capos were women who had been in Auschwitz some time and had shown ruthless leadership qualities. I think that the hut was divided lengthwise, but am not sure about this. At the bottom end of the hut there was a separate section with buckets, which was only open for use during the night.

There must have been some sort of importance or German magic in the number five because we were always in fives; perhaps because even the dumbest person can count to five on the fingers of one hand.

We were only allowed into the huts at night. The rest of the time we had to be out of doors, whatever the weather, and stay near to our hut, because one could never tell when the Germans might take it into their heads to call an *Appell*, when we had to line up in fives. It was a roll-call, when the total number of inmates was ascertained. There was not much to do, so *Appell* kept the Germans and us on our toes and it lasted a long time. We were not dismissed until everybody in the Auschwitz-Birkenau camp had been counted and the number agreed with that entered in the book.

On my first day there, I discovered that the Capos in our hut were Slovak and Czech. I took an early opportunity to tell them that I was also from Czechoslovakia, spoke Slovak and Czech and was only with the Hungarians – whom they despised – because I had escaped from the Germans into Hungary. Being Czechoslovakian was to my advantage. When the midday soup was doled out – having been brought in cauldrons by pyjama-clad men who, so I discovered, were the trustees and orderlies among the inmates – I addressed the Capo who was dishing it out in Slovak or Czech. The ladle went to the bottom of the cauldron and my soup contained a fair proportion of unidentifiable solids.

Every evening, after the last *Appell*, when we were locked into the hut, each person got a piece of blanket; speaking Slovak or Czech got me a bigger piece.

The Capos drew lines with white chalk along the floor of the hut. We slept in lines but there were so many women in the hut that the only way to sleep was like spoons, with one's head on the hip of the person in the row above. Otherwise there was not enough room for us all to lie down. We started to stack each other up from one end of the hut and lay down in sequence. If one person needed to turn over during the night it meant a major upheaval. If you had to visit the bucket during the night you were unlikely to find your place again unless your friends on either side were awake and were keeping the space for you. Otherwise you had to try to squeeze in somehow near the buckets, which made you very unpopular and it was also a very, very smelly place.

If it happened that your place was near the wall, you stood a better chance of getting it back, but then you had no hip to use as a cushion.

The Capos' status was way below that of the Germans but significantly above ours. They had a room of their own with bunk beds, had several blankets, first choice of the food available and complete control over the 250 women in each hut. They were maligned and hated but if they could not keep order they would be demoted, taken away, disappear and their replacement would be even keener and more brutal. I tried to keep in their good books without getting too close to them.

As far as our bodily functions went, a double row of

latrines ran between each set of two huts. There was, naturally, nothing to clean oneself with. If anybody showed signs of having a loose bowel action they were taken to the hospital hut, because there was an ever-present fear of typhus. They never returned.

Once a day we were pushed into the huts, when the pyjama-clad men came to take away the full buckets and replace them with empty ones. These latrines served two huts and one had to learn sphincter control while waiting for a seat to become available, hoping that an *Appell* would not be called before one had relieved oneself.

The only people who could talk to the pyjama-clad men, who were always accompanied by armed Germans, were the Capos and, as the men visited many parts of the camp, this was how news travelled.

That was how Ella, who was also in my hut and who knew that Gaby had been left with the grandparents in the train, found out that they had been gassed and that when Ferenc had found this out he made good his threat not to live if Gaby died by throwing himself on the electric fence.

It was how I found out that both my parents were also in Auschwitz, my mother in the adjoining site; but we never met.

One night, there was a commotion in the hut in the bucket section. I was in urgent need myself and went into the section where I found a girl lying on the ground and a doctor holding her hand and talking to her softly. There was a strong smell of acetone. The doctor whispered to me that the girl was a diabetic, already in a coma and that there was nothing we could do for her. She wasn't even certain whether the girl could still hear us.

'Should I tell the Capo?' I asked.

'No, let her be; she is in no pain. I'll tell her in the morning.'

In the morning the girl was carried by four women in a blanket to the hospital hut at the end of the compound. She was probably dead by then.

During the day it was very hot in the camp. There were no trees, no shade. We suffered seriously from thirst and dehydration.

Once a week we were marched out of the enclosed section, along a stony, dusty road to the Ablutions hut. We never knew whether the showers would be water or if we had been marched there to be gassed. The adjoining crematorium continually belched out noxious and obnoxious fumes. We were usually given a small piece of rough, grey soap – the unused portion of which had to be returned after the shower. There was no lather, the rumour was that it was made from human ashes and lye.

On the way we passed pools of stagnant water by the roadside. Some women were so thirsty, so crazed for a drink of water, that they broke ranks to kneel down and lap the water like dogs. The guards accompanying us yelled that the water was polluted, unfit to drink, would make us ill, but who cared by now?

Frequently we passed groups of gipsy women. They had not had their heads shaved. They wore their traditional headscarves and aprons of rough sacking. They were breaking stones making square cobbles. Talking was forbidden but occasionally someone felt brave enough to ask them where they came from: most of them were Romanian or Hungarian.

After the shower we got our garments back. Well, not actually the ones that we had worn on the way in but those of a previous group which had by now been sterilised and baked to board hardness. Obviously, nothing ever fitted and we started to prefer thick garments to thin ones, because the nights could be cold.

The Woman Without A Number

There were different kinds of *Appell* and we never knew which one was about to take place. There was the early morning, the midday and the evening ones, at each of which we were counted and re-counted. Then there was the *Appell* for the midday soup, when we saw the men approaching with the cauldrons and there was the Selection *Appell*, when we had to strip, put our clothes in a bundle in front of us and stand to attention. On a word of command we had to lift up the clothes above our heads. In our weakened state many started to wobble. Anybody who looked weak, too thin or appeared elderly was despatched to the gas chamber. Or maybe the strong ones were selected for labour. We never knew what the capricious brain of Dr Mengele and his staff had decided.

WE KEPT NO TRACK of time – each day was the same as the previous one, except for the one when we went for the showers and the change of clothes.

On one occasion after the showers, instead of the usual stiff garments which were thrown at us, we were given white blouses and dark skirts to wear, as well as sturdy shoes. What a surprise! Why? We wondered. Also, the crematorium stacks stood silent, no plume of smoke or smells emanated from them.

When we returned to our section of the camp, we found that several long tables had been put at the side of the hut where *Appell* normally was held and wooden benches and chairs were grouped around them. We were told to sit down and were each issued with a blank postcard and a pencil.

'Write home!' was the command.

Where was home? Who was at home?

I knew that my parents were here in Auschwitz, Marton was – God knows where – I doubted whether Gaspar was about or he would have come to Szekesfehervar and to write to Aunt Bella seemed futile. I thought of Marton's younger brother Laci and addressed the card to him. On the other side, using the smallest possible letters I started to write. This was going to be difficult, there was bound to be censorship.

'I am well,' I wrote, 'so is your cousin Ella.' I thought omission would tell him as much as confirmation.

A group of people approached. Dr Mengele and his staff were accompanying a prelate of the Catholic Church in his red Cardinal robes.

'He is a Papal Nuncio,' went the whisper. 'He is to report to the Pope on what he sees.'

He approached our table. I looked up briefly, caught his eye and looking down and turning to my neighbour said: *'Non credite quod videte; ecce non est veritatem.'* I dared a careful sideway glance. There seemed surprise in his eyes, he stretched out his hand, murmured a blessing carefully, not just over me, but over the whole group and making a point of blessing others at other tables.

My neighbour asked me what I had said. I told her that I had said, albeit in poor Latin, that he should not believe what he saw, that it was not the truth. I thought he had understood. I was doubtful whether it was of any use. I wondered whether Dr Mengele or his staff had realised what had happened. There was, fortunately, no come-back; I think they were too preoccupied to notice.

Shortly after he left, they collected the cards, the pencils, tables, benches and chairs. Sacks of old garments were brought; we were told to change quickly, that the blouses and skirts were needed elsewhere. It had all been a charade – for the benefit of the Pope's ambassador.

7

*

Appell

There were times when we were not on *Appell*, queuing for food or the toilets or being walked to and from ablutions. We sat in the sun, on the ground, leaning against the walls of the hut.

Early on, we made it a rule not to talk about our families – but talking of food and dreaming of it was permitted. Indeed, it could not be avoided. It stayed a favourite topic of conversation for most of us who survived. Oddly enough, we craved for very simple things – like a boiled potato or a nice, juicy apple.

One day I happened to mention that a gipsy had taught me how to read palms. I did not believe that one really could see the past and the future in the lines of a hand but it passed the time and I made sure that everybody got their allocation of at least two children, a lover or a husband, or possibly both. I explained, as it had been explained to me, what the various lines and marks on the palm represented and it became a matter of heated discussion when people found different interpretation to the same signs. I did not think that it caused any harm. Every so often, I saw a hand which gave me some concern but I always found other things to tell.

I shall never forget, however, when one day a girl, who managed to look beautiful even with a shaved head and rags on her back and who still looked the picture of health, asked me to read her hand. It was an unusual one. I asked her how old she was. She was just sixteen. The palm was smooth with hardly any signs and an extraordinarily short lifeline. Lifelines I refused to read, unless I could see that they were very long. There was literally nothing to tell from her hand, except for an early sudden death. I made up the usual rigmarole of a husband and two children and lots of travel but kept my eye on her after that. I was uneasy.

The next *Appell* was one where we were told to strip, bundle our clothes and lift the bundle in both hands above our heads. People seemed to be selected at random. Mengele and a woman officer had gone along the line and we, who had not been selected, heaved a sigh of relief – when that girl suddenly sneezed. Mengele's head swivelled round, he pointed at her and signed for her to step out and join the others who had been selected. They all went into the gas chamber. I refused to read any more palms after that.

We heard of people running to the wire and being electrocuted, of those being hanged, some skinned alive and their skins used to make lampshades and of medical experiments being carried out. We never heard any good news.

I awoke one morning and could not move. My left leg felt paralysed. My friends helped me to stand up but I could not move my leg or hip nor bend it at the knee. I was in agonising pain. If I could not stand at *Appell* I would be sent straight away to be gassed. They called the Capo.

'There is just one chance for her' the Capo said. 'Take her to the hospital.'

The Woman Without A Number

My friends laid me on a blanket, picked up the four corners and started to carry me there. We met some German guards on the way. They looked at me, shrugged their shoulders and pointed to the hospital. My friends left me there in the care of a Czech woman doctor. She examined me and said she could not find anything organically wrong, that perhaps a few days lying down might cure it. There was no medication.

The hospital was a dangerous place.

For most people there was only one way out – death – either from natural causes or as the result of experimentation. At the time, experiments were going on with X-rays. It seemed as if people were selected at random to be X-rayed – regardless of whether or not there was a need for it. It seemed random to us but probably not to the German doctor who was carrying it out. Most people were selected repeatedly to be X-rayed. I was X-rayed once but not having a number tattooed on my arm meant that they could not keep a check on me. When the German doctor asked for the woman without the number, the Czech doctor told him that I had died of meningitis. I was not the only one without a tattoo.

Every day the hospital was inspected and people who were very ill were selected and taken away, never to be seen again. There were several cases of meningitis in the hospital. The Germans thought that the disease was contagious and would not go near patients who had it or who had died from it. During the period of inspection, the Czech doctor put me into the middle of these patients – it was a relatively safe location from the Germans, but not from the disease.

After a few days my pains eased. The doctor told me that to be safe I would have to leave the hospital soon. In the meantime, I was given an armband and was now officially a nurse. After three days they managed to smuggle me back to my hut. This paralysis of my left leg has occurred from time to time since then, usually before travel or in times of extreme stress.

A couple of days later, when I didn't move quickly enough for a German soldier he hit me with a rifle butt across the shoulders.

My friends and I realised that if we stayed on in Auschwitz, sooner or later one or all of us would be selected to go into the gas chamber. Lack of food and, even more, of water was weakening all of us. We decided that we would go out with the next transport which would be sent to work.

About a week later at a selective *Appell*, Dr Mengele asked whether there were any doctors or nurses among us.

'This is it,' I said.

I was in the first line and stepped forward, to be followed by my friends. It was a risky thing to do, but we were going together – for better or worse. We were told to go to the side and to join some able-bodied women who had already been selected.

IT WAS NOW THE end of July 1944. We were marched away and this time it was much further than the normal showering/disinfecting block. We were herded into a large, empty room, told to strip and pushed into a shower room. By now we were used to this. After the shower we were pushed into another large room, which was divided by a long counter, behind which stood women in striped uniforms and behind them were mountains of clothes. We were told to approach the counter in fives and to move along. We were each issued with two pairs of white cotton knickers, two white cotton vests, a woollen dress, a warm woollen coat, on the back of which was a streak of yellow paint, still quite tacky, a night shift of blue gingham flannel, a towel, a piece of soap and a blanket. We were fitted with a pair of stout shoes and given a canvas bag and an enamel mug. Thus loaded we were pushed into the next room, told to dress, to put our 'belongings' in the bag.

We were given some more substantial soup than usual and then told to bed down for the night. We managed to get near to the top wall and got into our, now usual, spoon pattern to go to sleep. There was more room here than in the blocks.

Before I managed to get to sleep two young girls in striped pyjamas, aged about twelve crawled over to me. They were twins whom I had fleetingly known in Szekesfehervar. They told me that, being twins, they had not been put into the gas chamber but were being used for experiments – different substances were being injected into them. They also told me that they had seen their own parents being pushed into the gas chamber. They finished by telling me, 'You are leaving this place; you are going to live, but we are not. Once they finished experimenting on us twins, they will send us to the gas chamber. Remember what you have seen here and tell the world about it, because we will not be able to do so.'

It has taken me a long time to be able to do this.

The next morning we were given a hunk of bread and a drink of water and were then taken to the railway siding and put into cattle trucks. There was some straw there, but the guards who were going with us made us pile it up in one corner and then put their own haversacks on it. 'This is our place,' they said 'you keep well away from it.'

We did.

Eventually all 530 of us were entrained, the guards swung themselves up into the trucks and we were off. The journey took three days. The train stopped and started, went forward and backwards – there seemed to be the sound of gunfire nearly all the time. Whenever we were stopped the guard slid open the door, but warned us not to go out. Eventually he did let us go out, one by one, accompanied by a guard, to relieve ourselves. The hunk of bread we had brought with us had been eaten long ago and the half barrel in the corner, which had been full of water, was now dry. We were hungry and thirsty and so were the guards. They had also finished the rations they had brought in their haversacks.

On the second night the train stopped near a station. The guards again opened the door. Their sergeant came from the front of the train and consulted with them. Then he walked to the station. About half an hour later big cauldrons of hot pea soup were being trundled along.

'All right,' said the guard, as he was given a beaker of soup, 'there is enough for everybody here.' So there was. Our mugs were filled with the best food we had been given since our arrival in Auschwitz.

At dawn we continued our journey. After we had shared the soup with the guards we realised that life had taken a turn for the better.

WE ARRIVED AT LIPPSTADT on the fourth day. A camp site had been prepared for us. It was a hutment for slave labour inside a high wire enclosure. Each hut had several rooms with three-tiered bunks and, at the end of each, was a washroom with showers and long troughs with taps for washing. We five were told to go to the first hut just inside the gate: this was the hospital hut. 'Make a Revier,' was the order. In German military language a Revier was a sickbay. Since ours was not only a sickbay but also acted as a clinic, pharmacy, medical and nurses' quarters, I referred to it then, and still do, as a 'hospital'.

The Woman Without A Number

The first room on the left, which faced the gate, was to be our bedroom. There were two single beds and two double bunks in it, with a straw-filled mattress in each. The doctors had the single beds, we the bunks.

There were several rooms on each side of a long corridor running down the middle and the usual washing facilities at the end. The first room opposite to ours was comparatively small, so it was decided to make that the 'isolation room'. The next one was large and became the clinic. The one opposite was to be the operating theatre and the other rooms were fitted with single beds as wards. Naturally, before anything could be done we had to have an *Appell* – just to check that nobody had gone missing on the journey. No, we were all there, all 530 of us. We were mostly Hungarians until a second transport of about 300 women joined us in November. In that group were women of French, Dutch, Slovak, Greek and Romanian nationality.

We were being guarded by members of the *Wehrmacht*, the German Army. There were a couple of female officers. The others, except for the Guard Commandant, were either very young or rather old and decrepit.

The Guard Commandant decided that there had to be a person in charge of each hut. These he picked at random from people who could speak German. I was put in charge of the hospital hut. He then told us that there was also to be one person in overall charge of us and Ella, my cousin, was chosen. That proved to be rather useful for all of us – she and I managed to finesse around the Germans on several occasions.

Next to our camp there was a huge torpedo-shaped bunker for the German officers and soldiers and slit trenches had been dug in front of our huts for us to use in case of air raids. Next to the bunker was a large factory, which produced all kinds of weaponry from hand grenades to bombs, from machine gun bullets to anti-tank weapons. On the other side of the factory were camps of Russian prisoners of war, who, contrary to the Geneva Convention, were made to work in the armament factory. The railway line on which we had arrived and which was also used to take the manufactured products away ran between our enclosure and the factory.

I was given a piece of paper and a pencil and was told to help the doctors make a list, in German, of the things we needed in the hospital – not that there was a guarantee that we would get them, as things were in short supply even for Germans.

I can't remember everything we got but we had an autoclave, forceps and scalpels, lint and rolls of gauze, which we made into swabs and sterilised, thermometers, temperature charts, spatulas, needles and catgut, crepe paper bandages and elastoplast as well as a pink antiseptic solution and iodine. It had been a long time since fabric bandages were seen in Germany. Medicines were mainly aspirin, codeine, cough mixtures and tannin tablets. There was also Vaseline and a couple of ointments and we had some spare blankets. But we had no hypodermic syringes until much later. We settled in. Those in the factories worked in two twelve-hour shifts, from six until six. We worked as the need arose, besides having a clinic at the end of each shift.

WHEN THE WORKERS AT the armament factory left or returned to camp there was *Appell*. The outgoing workers were counted first and, naturally, they had to march in fives. The incoming ones then had to line up - also in fives - and be counted back before being allowed to have food and go to bed.

The patients were only rarely counted. Even when, on

the odd occasion, the Guard Commandant and one or other of the SS women came into the hospital, they would not enter the isolation room. If we offered to open the door, we were told to desist. That proved to have advantages.

At *Appell* the first thing the guards did was to go through the huts and make certain that there was nobody there. However, as they went from one hut to the next, there was nobody to check that someone, in dire need to relieve themselves, had not rushed back into one of the huts that had already been searched. The hut commandants were supposed to stop it, but then, we were not inhuman.

The agreement was that if that happened, the person had to remain inside because there was hell to pay if someone emerged from a hut that had already been searched. It meant that the whole *Appell* had to be restarted, including recall of the workers from the factory. Standing in the dark and – often – the rain, after working for twelve hours, getting wetter and hungrier was not exactly popular.

Since the guards rarely entered the hospital and the Commandant relied on me to tell him how many people were in the hospital hut, Ella and I had devised a system to make the numbers always tally.

While the guards were searching the huts the hut commandants and Ella did a preliminary count of those standing outside. She had been with the guards when they counted the workers going out, so she knew how many were supposed to be left inside the camp. Having counted everybody and while the guards were in the last hut before they came to the hospital, I called over to her in Hungarian, '*Mennyi kell?*' How many do you need? The number required then became that of the patients and staff in the hospital hut. I acquired the nickname 'Mennikell', which naturally the Germans could not understand.

I spent my twenty-first birthday in the camp. It was a

memorable day, one I shall never forget. Besides being forbidden to do any work and told to relax, I also received presents. Some of the girls worked in the aluminium section of the factory and they produced, from scraps, a necklace with a medallion spelling out my name. They also cut and engraved a small fat book with a spiral binding, the pages made from temperatures charts, which was the only paper we could get hold of. In it was the signature of every person in the camp. It was all miniaturised, the book was only about three centimetres by two, and one needed a magnifying glass to read the names and the messages. In the evening there was a party, a lot of singing and a birthday cake made from slices of bread, spread with margarine and jam – many must have gone without their special rations – with the requisite number of candles made of aluminium. Nobody, but nobody, not even the richest person in the world, could have had a more special birthday. I treasured the necklace and the book and took them with me everywhere, but somehow, somewhere, along my many moves in England, they both disappeared.

The guards around the camp were elderly *Wehrmacht* conscripts. The main gate was near to the hospital hut and I would often go over and talk to the elderly soldier who was on guard duty there. To me he seemed ancient, grey and wrinkled, small and shrunk – he was probably in his sixties. He often used to grumble, saying he could not see what the world had come to that had taken him from the office chair where he had sat through his life to stand now by a gate for a whole day. He had been happy working in the bank and well looked after by his Jewish boss. Life had been much easier then.

Sometimes he stood with his back to the gate, lit a cigarette and then put his hands behind his back for me to take it. This had to be done carefully and I had then to go quickly to the back of the hut to smoke the cigarette so that neither of us could be caught.

On my birthday, when I walked to the gate, the hand behind his back contained not one lit cigarette, but a packet of ten and a box of matches – both incredibly valuable presents. My hand-rolled cigarettes usually consisted of crepe paper bandage smoothed out and filled with chopped up leaves. It was a horrible cigarette, it made me and all other smokers cough, but it was a smoke.

By this time, air raids were frequent. If the sirens went off, the factory was evacuated. The workers came back into the camp, the Germans went into the bunker and we were supposed to go into the slit trenches which had been dug in the ground in front of the huts. Naturally, we didn't. If the weather was fine – and it usually was in the case of daytime air raids - blankets were spread on the ground outside and people sat or lay around. The Commandant stood at the entrance of the bunker and shouted and was hopping mad, but we really could not care less. If we saw any planes, we waved to them, although I don't suppose we were really seen. If we were, the airmen would have wondered why we were not in bunkers, but enjoying the sunshine. Somehow, we did not think that we were vulnerable – by now we were certain that we would live.

When the bombing raids continued during the night and the nearby towns were hit, the Commandant asked for volunteers to come and help with moving debris. If it was a nice day, many offered because it got us out from the camp, and passing bricks from one to another was not really such hard work. The main emphasis was always on getting the roadways clear. We worked alongside the German inhabitants, mainly women and children. Those of us who could speak German talked to them about how the war was going and how long it would last. I must admit that our main aim was to see the damage the allied bombers had done; we felt that the more, the nearer our day of salvation.

The only other way to get out of the camp was if someone had toothache. Then, accompanied by a guard, the person with the toothache was allowed to walk into town and visit the dentist – and bring back news into the camp. The dentist was a kind man; he often prescribed a lengthy course of treatment, which needed frequent visits to him, particularly, if the patient was pretty. I only managed one visit to the dentist; my teeth were in too good a condition. I had no fillings or cavities and that they were loose was due to malnutrition, a condition from which everybody was then suffering.

8

*

Life And Death In Camp

According to Regulations – and everything in Germany was governed strictly and entirely by regulations – female workers in the factory were entitled to 3,000 calories per day. That consisted of a slab of black bread, issued in the morning, together with 'coffee' made, I think, from roasted acorns but then the Germans did not get anything better either and, at midday, a sort of thick soup. In the evening, there was more coffee and 'Zulage'; something to spread on your bread, which could be either margarine or jam made from carrots or a small piece of cheese or a spoonful of sugar and sometimes even meat paste. These items were issued in bulk to each hut and were distributed by the hut commandant. The quantity was, naturally, governed by regulations. A slab of margarine was for twenty – with careful slicing, it was possible to make twenty-two portions and that meant that in a hut for 200, the hut commandant had half a slab at her disposal. Jam and sugar were by the level spoonful – there was not much leeway there, cheese was also sliced like the margarine. Since I never had a sweet tooth I always exchanged my jam and sugar for extra cheese. Jam and sugar were more popular, so the exchange rate favoured me.

The quality of the soup gradually deteriorated and eventually became inedible. Ella, the hut commandants and I got together. We felt something had to be done because people couldn't face eating the soup, even when really hungry, and were pouring it away and getting weaker. We knew that the cooks were German and that they were probably using some of the ingredients meant for us for themselves.

We did not think that telling the Commandant that the cooks were stealing the food allocated to us would be particularly popular – it would probably antagonise him and, so far, he had not been menacing.

'What' someone ventured, 'if we got him to taste what they bring us?'

'Yes, but what, if being German, he likes it?'

'He can't, he can't' said others.

'There is no way we can be certain about this.'

We pondered.

'We could say that, as Hungarians, our way of cooking is different. Could we ask for Hungarian food?'

This was an audacious suggestion but we worked out a strategy. We would first of all explain to him, that, since all of us were Hungarians, we were used to a completely different type of food, indeed, could not really eat other food. It had to contain paprika. We then had to ask him to taste it, so that he could see for himself that there was no paprika in it. It was thought that, as my German was best, it should be me. Next day, when the Commandant marched in, followed by the cauldrons of soup, I stepped forward, as I normally would, to collect the soup for the patients, but instead I addressed him.

'Sir, I am sorry, but there is a serious problem with the food,' I said.

'How so?'

'We are having more and more people coming to the hospital with stomach pains and loose bowels. It is the wrong kind of food for them. Hungarians are used to food cooked with lots of paprika and that keeps their insides in order. Please, taste the soup, you will see that there is no paprika in it. Also, it is so watery, that it goes straight through them and they get no nourishment from it. Before long, we shall have so many people ill that there will not be enough fit workers for the factory.'

The Commandant took a ladle and asked what soup it was supposed to be. He was told potato.

He dipped the ladle into the soup and fished around in the liquid.

'Where are the potatoes?' he asked.

The men, who had brought the cauldrons of soup, shrugged their shoulders. The Commandant took a mouthful and promptly spat it out. 'This is not even fit for pigs. I'll deal with it.'

The next day Ella and I were called to the Commandant. 'I have made a decision. I want you to select five women who are good cooks. They will be the cooks for your camp in future.' And so it was.

Ella found five cooks who were marched off separately in the morning to the kitchens of the factory. The food improved dramatically. There were now potatoes, vegetables and, sometimes, even meat in the soup. On Sundays, we had sauerkraut with lumps of fat meat in it; sometimes there were even dumplings in the soup. People could work on that diet but it was too good to last, though.

There were just enough non-Hungarians in the camp to complain that they could not eat all this paprika and after a few weeks the cooks were returned to camp. They were more valuable as factory workers. The German cooks came back but the soup was a little bit thicker than before and did contain the odd potato.

IT MUST HAVE BEEN at the end of November when another transport of three hundred women joined us from Auschwitz, among them was my cousin, twice removed, Iby Foldes. They brought news about other camps, like Bergen-Belsen and Buchenwald. They also brought typhoid with them. Within a couple of days we had three cases. This had to be reported to the Commandant. Panic ensued. This was serious, it could spread also to the Germans.

We now had eight cases, and more came along by the day. Eventually there were over twenty, and the isolation room could only accommodate four people. A little distance from ours, was an isolation camp for workers suffering from infectious diseases. It was only opened as and when it was needed; there was no resident medical staff. The Commandant wanted one doctor and one nurse to volunteer to go with the patients suffering from typhoid.

We had had a change of doctors since we arrived. The dentist did not want to work as a doctor any more and preferred to work in the factory. That brought us below complement. We asked Ella to find out whether, by chance, there was a medical person among the workers and there was. She was much older than us, probably well over forty and it was quite extraordinary that she had survived the selections in Auschwitz. She had been a researcher in oncology and agreed to work in the clinic with us. It was she who offered to go with the patients. As a child I had had paratyphoid and I thought that I was probably immune, so I volunteered as well.

We were transported to this small camp in a horse-drawn wagon. It was really only one hut with six rooms with the

105

usual ablution facilities. It was set within an enclosure of high wire fencing and behind big, padlocked gates. In one of the rooms there were three Polish girls suffering from advanced TB.

With the twenty typhus patients, among them my cousin Iby, we also brought a French girl whom we had been hiding from the Germans and from work in the factory. She was small and slight and had a wound on her leg that had refused to heal. She could not stand for any length of time and was therefore unable to work. We had been moving her from room to room, in and out of the isolation room for weeks now.

Any patients who did not recover quickly were sent away from the labour camp to Bergen-Belsen where people died very quickly. We tried to prevent this. She and we agreed that the danger of catching typhus was an option to be preferred.

The only suitable medications we could take with us were tannin, digitalis and an opium solution, as well as antiseptics.

It was winter, it was cold. There were iron stoves in the rooms. We used three rooms for the patients, putting eight in each room, trying to have a mix of seriously and not so ill.

I managed to get quantities of rather dusty coal and some kindling. We kept the stoves going day and night. There was not much else we could do. We kept the patients warm and clean and gave them lots of boiled water to drink into which we put a few drops of opium solution.

Food for us – that is, the Polish girls, the doctor and me, was left at the gate. The Germans did not think that the patients would survive and did not need therefore to be fed. After a few days I explained to them that we did need food for the patients if they were to survive and be able to work again but not the usual food of the camp. Each day I told them what I needed for the next and was given, to my amazement, what I requested: cooked semolina or plain boiled potatoes, once even a clear meat broth. The patients gradually improved. To keep their spirits up I told them stories, got them to sing their favourite songs and devised games. As they got better some of them could help with the stoves and with the feeding of those who were still poorly. Against the odds all of them started to recover, except the doctor who was getting frailer and frailer. She told me that she had cancer and that there was really not a lot that could be done for her. I think that most of the opium solution was used by her.

At Christmas we were still in isolation. A few of the patients were still not well enough to work and, as far as the Commandant was concerned, either all of us stayed out or we came back together into the camp. For Christmas dinner the cooks provided the traditional pork and sauerkraut. That caused a problem. The doctor and I knew that the patients would be looking forward to having such a special meal but the fatty meat was bound to have an adverse effect on their fragile innards and cause diarrhoea. The doctor and I decided to take out the meat, cut off the fat, put the lean pieces back into the cabbage and serve it. The fat we cut off we put into a separate bowl and on the windowsill outside our room. We had no idea what we would do with it eventually. Our room was always locked if one of us was not in it, on account of the opium solution we kept there and to which the Polish girls were evidently addicted. It was really cold outside and it never entered our minds that someone would willingly and voluntarily go out into the cold.

We served the meal, giving the Polish girls some fatty pieces in their cabbage. We had ours with the patients and spent time with them talking of Christmases past and what we would do at them in the future. When it got dark we returned to our room. I had forgotten all about the fat outside the window. We were woken up during the night. Several of the patients had violent diarrhoea. We were very worried, because we thought they'd had a relapse and that further weeks of isolation and nursing lay ahead until one of them admitted what had happened.

They had gone out of the hut and had seen on our windowsill the bowl of fatty bits and thought that we had kept the best parts for ourselves. So they took some of it and ate it.

I don't think I had ever, or since, been so angry. I told them I felt like letting them stew in their own mess; having spent weeks nursing them and cleaning up after them. To have it all undone by their greed and thoughtlessness was more than I could face. Did they not realise how carefully they had been led and fed back to health? Did they not realise that their insides were so delicate that they had to be careful for a long time about what they ate? A relapse like this could kill them. Did they really think that I had removed the fat for myself? If so, they could go and have what they had not yet taken, it was all still there. 'Eat it and look after each other as best you can, because I shall ask the guards when they come in the morning to let me and the doctor go back to the camp.' I stormed out.

Needless to say, the doctor and I stayed. We had no further problems with them. The Polish girls died quietly a short time after Christmas. We told the guards. They were taken away and I was told that all their belongings were to be burned to prevent the spread of infection. I burned everything except for a red satin petticoat and the feathers out of one pillow and a piece of a sheet. Out of the sheet I drew the threads and used them to embroider the beginning of the Brahms Lullaby, *Guten Abend, gut Nacht*, on the red satin. I made a cushion out of it and filled it with feathers.

I really hated one of the German women guards, who was always making fun of us, of our shorn heads, of our efforts to make ourselves look respectable. When we went back to the camp – this time the journey was on foot – we passed the German guard quarters. I knew which was her room and the window was open. As I went past, I threw the cushion in. I hoped she'd get TB and die – soon.

The next day she asked whether anyone knew anything about an embroidered cushion. I told her that I had made it. She just grinned and shook her head. Eventually I did get my revenge on her for her jibes about our shorn heads.

WE ALL CEASED TO menstruate within a short time of arriving in Auschwitz. It was not therefore possible to find out whether anybody was pregnant. Any woman arriving in Auschwitz obviously pregnant was sent straight to the gas chamber.

On arriving at the slave labour camp in Lippstadt, it became obvious that some women were pregnant. We did not know whether this would also be a life-threatening condition here, so every effort was made to hide a pregnancy. Two of the women wished their pregnancies to be terminated – and this was done with help from the doctors.

Since one or two of the women in each hut had the task of keeping the ablutions clean and did not work in the factory, this job was, by common consent, allocated to the remaining two heavily pregnant women and at *Appell* they were always put into a middle row.

When it came to the time of delivery, the doctor decided that it would be better if this did not take place in the hospital. Ella's room was to be the delivery room and only the doctors were to be present. Each woman was delivered of a healthy child. It was not possible to hide from the Germans that there were suddenly babies in the camp. The Commandant was amazed at how we had managed to keep it hidden from him. He agreed that the mothers could continue to work in the camp rather than go to work in the factory; after all, it made no difference who stayed back, as long as the right number of people worked in the factory. That was what caused trouble.

According to some regulation no more than five per cent of the work force of 850 was allowed to be off work which was forty-two people. In this number were included Ella, the two doctors and three nurses at the hospital, the two hut cleaners and all the patients who were bedridden in the hospital. It was a continuing battle to maintain this figure.

According to the Germans, if a person had a temperature below 38 degrees they had to go to work, they were not sick enough to stay in the hospital. Patients soon became adept in rubbing up the thermometer or dipping it in hot liquid - the latter was a much more fallible method as the temperature tended to go too high. If there were not many in-patients, we turned a blind eye to this, because everybody was tired from the long shifts, especially those on the night shift. I think that, eventually, the Commandant must have thought it odd that we rarely had fewer than thirty-four in-patients.

Sad to say, there was always the odd person who would try to curry favour with the Germans and tell tales. Thus it came about that, at the beginning of March, I was hauled up before the Commandant for 'sabotaging the war effort' by keeping people in hospital who were fit to work. It was true – but who would have done otherwise? Our daily surgeries, held when the shifts came off work, had progressively more and more cases of work-related injuries. In one instance, a person was scalped by the blade of a machine because they had failed to replace the safety guard. There were obvious signs of exhaustion and, in such cases if at all possible, we took a person in for a couple of days' sleep.

My punishment was that I would no longer be in charge of the hospital but would have to work in the factory and on continuous night shift. I also had to move from the comparative comfort of the hospital hut to a bunk in one of the others. By this time, work in the factory went on in fits and starts. Frequently, there was no material; the cast iron rods which came in for processing were full of imperfections and there were air raids nearly every day and most nights.

I was put on a machine that made machine gun bullets; or rather, I had to file the rusty bits of the bullets that had been cast. From me, they went to a German control. Any that were too loose for the shell casing were discarded and sent to be melted down. The quality of the metal was very poor. If I conscientiously removed every bit of rust then all the bullets were too small. If I did not, then they were discarded as dangerous. There was a certain level of tolerance which we were supposed to apply, but I regularly went beyond it. Before long, my colleagues beside me cottoned on to what I was doing and all did the same. The Germans just grumbled that the material they sent to the factory was getting worse and worse. No blame was attached to us.

There was a certain amount of work for each machine to achieve in any one shift. I found that if I worked fast for a couple of hours, I could have a sit down or even a lie-down for half an hour or so at the back of the workshop – ostensibly I had gone to the loo. The German workers, all women, were not unfriendly and shouted a warning if a supervisor came along. After all, they did the same. By now, they were not taking the war effort very seriously. My spare time was spent with my friends in the hospital.

Putting me to work in the factory was part of a desperate drive to improve efficiency. The day before I had to start in the factory some cattle trucks arrived on the railway line just outside the camp, where usually flat wagons delivered the rods of cast iron. With the trucks came a detachment of soldiers, who were not of the more relaxed type of our camp guards.

All persons who were chronically ill, feeble or unable to work – which included the two nursing mothers – were to be transported to a more suitable location – to Bergen-Belsen. On this occasion the Commandant came into the hospital and selected those among the patients who appeared to him to be either injured or unlikely to be working within days. He also asked to see the records to establish whether any of the patients had been there longer than one week.

We had always tried to discharge patients after a week and to readmit them a day or so later, in order to show that we had no seriously ill patients. This was not always practical, especially in the case of severe work injuries. The danger of sick people being transported away to Bergen-Belsen was very real. On this occasion the Commandant was much sterner than usual, obviously trying to impress the visitors or having been reprimanded.

Straw was placed in the bottom of the trucks. The mothers with their babies climbed up. One of them made a comparatively comfortable bed for hers near to the sliding doors, while she helped others up. When all the sick were in the truck, one of the soldiers swung himself up and, in the process, inadvertently or intentionally, crushed the baby with his heavily shod boot. There was a stunned silence before the mother snatched up the crushed, bleeding infant and let out a scream.

The soldier said, 'What are you screaming about? I probably saved your life. If the child's alive when we get there both of you go into the gas chamber. Now you might have a chance to live.'

The French girl with the suppurating wound in her leg was also taken. I heard some time after the war that the woman whose child had been killed, had indeed survived, as had her husband and that they had been reunited.

THEN, ONE DAY, THERE was ominous quiet – we realised that we could not hear any noise from the factory. It had been some days since any iron rods had arrived on the siding.

Every day and every night we seemed to spend more time inside the enclosure rather than in the factory. Work had slowed down, it was nearly at a stand-still. The German control staff spent more time smoking and chatting than checking the products. Some of the machines, which had been breaking down more and more often, were not even started up.

The Guard Commandant called an *Appell*. We were told that we were to leave camp the next evening and, since all the people who were sick had already been moved by rail, we would have to go on foot. We should take nothing with us – not that we had a lot.

Most of us agreed that it would be best if we put on whatever clothes we had. It was early in the spring, the weather was changeable and it could be very cold at night.

In the evening, there was the usual *Appell*. The guards produced a large handcart, on which they had put their belongings and also some supplies of food, as well as a Soyer boiler. Twelve women were selected; six to pull the cart, six to push it. We were told that this would be done in shifts.

The doctors had packed up some medical supplies in a bag and put that also on the handcart. Nobody seemed to notice that they had done so. We set off. I do not know in which direction we went but after we left the debris-ridden streets of the town we walked all night through flat, agricultural land. The Soyer boiler was set up, filled with water and we got some dry bread and 'ersatz' coffee, brewed from dried acorns. We were footsore and tired, fell asleep in the hay and slept all day.

As it got dark we started off again. If one person fell behind unable to keep up, one of the guards detached himself from us and stayed with that straggler. A little later a shot was heard and the guard reappeared.

On the second night, people who found it difficult to keep up were hoisted up by their friends onto the handcart, which was now pulled and pushed by many more women than the original twelve and also had by now less food on it. The threat of being shot if one could not keep up was as good a deterrent as the rifle butts that were used freely by the guards to keep us in line and moving.

The second morning, we again got some dry bread and 'ersatz' coffee, before settling in barns to sleep. We felt that we were actually going round in circles – there did not seem to be any special direction; we trundled along country lanes, between fields of turnips which were piled up in clumps covered with soil, but we could see them protruding from the side. Turnips were cattle food but we were so hungry, that several women broke rank, ran down to the clumps, took a couple of turnips and ran back again. We brushed off the soil and bit into the flesh – passing the turnip back and forth along our line. The guards yelled that we would get sick from eating raw turnips; we replied that since we had nothing else to eat and we were hungry, what did it matter?

On the third morning I could not get up. My left leg had again gone lame. My friends said that no way was I going on the cart, no way would they say anything to the guards, but we would manage. Two of them joined their arms behind me, I put my arms over their shoulders and so we went along, hobbling, but still keeping up somehow.

By now the guards had put their own packs on the cart, to make it easier for them to walk. At the end of that night's march the guards could not find any barns for us to shelter in. There was a little wood and that is where we stayed, shivering in the cold.

As dawn broke we heard the continuous drone of aircraft and the thump of bombs falling in the distance. We consoled ourselves with the thought that the Allies would soon find us.

The German guards huddled together. They decided that we were in a very vulnerable position and would have to walk on, even if it was daylight now. As we started off, the drone of aircraft grew louder and with it came also the distant noise of vehicles and of gunfire. Church bells were ringing. The guards shouted at us to get into the ditches that ran alongside the roads. We did as we were ordered. The land was flat here. The planes came in low over us and in the distance we could now see tanks, each covered with a large pink sheet and the village houses in the distance suddenly sprouted white flags. We noticed that the guards were inching their way, on their stomachs, back into the woods, away from us.

The whisper went round, it's the Allies. Some brave souls jumped up and started to run towards the tanks. Braver ones surrounded the guards, who had by now thrown away their rifles because it was easier and faster to crawl backwards without them. The rifles were found and the guards were held at gunpoint. I stayed in the ditch – I could not move.

The tanks came along, they were not British, but American. We had been caught in the pincer movement the allied forces were making around the Ruhr. They must have been amazed to find themselves surrounded by cheering gaunt women with short hair and in clothes with a broad yellow stripe on the back.

The Woman Without A Number

The American commandant told us that they were not staying but moving on and clearing a corridor and that there were still German forces either side of us. They told us that we were in charge for the next three days, when forces to occupy this area would arrive. Until then, they said, 'Do whatever you like, what you feel needs doing. Nobody is going to ask any questions.'

A secure cellar was found in one of the village houses. The German guards were herded in. But first, the woman guard who had mocked our shorn heads was sat on a chair in the middle of the village and her long blond locks were cut off and then her head was shaved. The only audience was us – no German showed his face outside.

I was carried by my friends to a nearby farmhouse that showed a white flag. An old farmer with a woman and a little girl were sitting at the table having breakfast, pretending that what went on outside had nothing to do with them, and I was put on a settee near the fireplace. My doctor friend warned me to be very careful what I ate, because our insides would be very fragile after the period of malnourishment.

'No milk,' she said. I did not need to be told that, I knew I could not drink milk. They were going to find accommodation for us, because having looked at this house, they realised that it only had that one room. The woman whispered something to the little girl. I wondered what they thought of me, lying there on their settee, thin and haggard, with very short hair and a coat with a broad yellow streak at the back.

The little girl slid off the bench on which she had been sitting. She reached over to the centre of the table and picked something up. She came over to me and offered me a dark brown egg.

'It's Easter Sunday,' she said.

PART FOUR

9

*

Building Bridges

Time seemed unimportant now. Contrary to friends, I felt
no desire to go back home; I felt certain that there was
nobody waiting for me. I felt that it did not matter where I
was or what was to happen to me. There was no euphoria –
no joy.

The next weeks are hazy – I remember that my doctor
friends found an empty house and we moved into it. I still
could not move my left leg, there was no pain, I just could not
move it. The doctor had no idea what to do and nor did I.

The area was occupied by the Americans. We were
supplied with large quantities of K rations – wooden boxes
full of canned food but without the means of opening them,
we had to 'requisition' a crowbar and a can opener.

We were not the only ones to be liberated. There had
been a Russian Prisoner of War Camp nearby and before
long the improvised surgery in our house was frequented by
many of them with broken noses and other minor injuries,
acquired as a result of a sudden availability of German
alcohol. Nobody had any money – we all lived by barter. So,

to show their appreciation the Russian soldiers 'liberated' a statue of the Virgin and Christ from the local church and brought it to us. They were promptly told to take it back where it belonged. It was not considered to be suitable payment for Jewish doctors.

American soldiers, mainly officers, started to visit us and bring food, cigarettes, coffee and alcoholic drinks. We were not used to the latter – and the addition of pineapple juice made even the strongest German spirits palatable; indeed we were not aware that we were drinking them – often with disastrous results.

Among the 700 or so women in our camp were three Dutch girls. After a week, when the Americans told us that there was no longer a German army between us and the Atlantic, the girls 'liberated' three bicycles and set off to cycle home. We remonstrated with them about the distance and uncertainty, but they were adamant. They were so determined that I would not be surprised if they reached their hometown.

There is only one vivid memory of this time and that is because I have a photograph of it. A few days after being liberated, we were all collected in a large room – I think it was the school – for a thanksgiving service; commemorating being alive. A day or so later, I was visited by the American Jewish chaplain. He gave me an American Army Jewish prayer book, inserted a dedication and his name and address in the States.

'If you decide to come to the States, contact me. I'll be there for you,' he said.

I can remember that prayer book lying with other personal possessions in a box when we moved to Leeds but I cannot find it or the prayer book now.

Ironically, we effectively set up a sort of camp in this little town of Kaunitz. It was designated as an open DPC

(Displaced Persons' Camp) and we were helped by UNRRA (United Nations Relief and Rehabilitation Administration).

My leg was no better and I was getting more and more depressed about it. My doctor friends consulted the American medic who thought I should go into a German hospital. I agreed, provided I was not going on my own. The thought of being surrounded only by Germans was something I could not countenance. Trust was not a feeling I had towards them. Alice, a Hungarian woman whose eczema was worsening rather than improving was to accompany me. The next day we were put into an Army Jeep and taken to the hospital in, I think, Bielefeld. We went just as we were, with what we stood up in, since we owned nothing. When we arrived, the nuns who were the nurses in the hospital put us in hospital nightclothes. I asked them, please, to burn the clothes I had on.

'What? Everything?' they queried.

'No, I'll keep the shoes and the coat.'

I can't remember the next days or weeks, I think I had injections and massage and eventually my leg regained its sense of feeling and I could move. With that returned also my will to live. I realised that my stay in the hospital was not to be permanent and that I would have to face whatever awaited me in the world.

I now asked for needles, thread and scissors. When the nun asked what I was going to do with it I told her, 'I think this coat is too good to be thrown away, you can see that it was made with care and love but it has been disfigured by the broad yellow stripe painted down the back. It was put there to shame us. There is no way I can remove the paint without damaging the coat. I shall unpick the coat and turn it inside out. It will be serviceable and only I shall know that on the inside there is a yellow streak, just to remind me that the shame is not on me but on those who put it there.'

The Woman Without A Number

She brought me a small pair of scissors, two needles, telling me to be careful with them because they were hard to come by and a reel of black cotton.

'What will you wear under this coat,' she asked. 'I have burned the other things you wore.'

'If I have nothing else I'll be naked, but I would never again have worn those rags,' I replied defiantly.

During the next few days she often came to my room and saw me unpicking the lining and then the coat itself. She told me that I could use the iron in the laundry room. I put the coat together again, having undone and redone even the set-in pockets. I invisibly mended the buttonholes with thread pulled from the selvedge, a skill I learned in the dressmaking classes I had attended during one summer holiday while I was still at school. I then sewed in the lining and replaced the buttons. After pressing, the coat was as good as new – of dark blue cloth with a faint red check in it.

The next day the nun brought me an old sheet, which had already been turned – sides to middle – and a badly frayed grey blanket, which was threadbare in places.

'We can't give you any clothes, we only have our habits and a count is kept on all linen and blankets here. But these have been thrown away as being of no further use, you might be able to make something out of them.'

I thanked her.

'I do need some bigger scissors and white thread, please' I said.

Out of the blanket I cut a pair of trousers and a short bolero-style jacket. There was not enough fabric for sleeves. From the sheet I cut two blouses and two pairs of knickers. Buttons or zips were non-existent, so the knickers were held up with drawstrings. The blouses had v-necks with a small collar and short sleeves. The biggest problem was how to hold up the trousers. I devised a front panel, like an apron. To the top of each side, I sewed long strips and put loops at the waist. The strips went through the loops and were tied at the back. At the front it looked as if there were two pockets.

When the outfits were ready I put them on and went on my first walk out of the hospital with Alice. Her eczema had improved considerably. The doctor had told me that I could leave the hospital whenever I wished – after all, I could now walk.

To our surprise we saw soldiers in different uniforms – British soldiers. I asked one of them where their headquarters was. We had to find out what was going to happen to us. Alice was keen to go home and to find her husband; I was, oddly, still reluctant to contemplate a return home. It had been a long time since I had been at home, I had been through a lot in the last three years and I dreaded the thought of returning and finding myself alone in familiar surroundings. Better to be a stranger in a foreign country and start a new life, to cut off the past.

We were directed to the local HQ of the British forces. On entering the house I was surprised to meet one of my fellow captives, a Hungarian girl who spoke English and acted as their interpreter. Alice told her that she wanted to go home and that was easily solved. The DP camp commandant was contacted and Alice was told that she would be collected from the hospital and taken back there, transport to Hungary was due to go shortly.

I told her that I did not want to go back to the camp. My English was fluent as was my German. I also spoke French, Czech, Slovak and Hungarian and some Russian. I enquired if there was any chance of my working as an interpreter.

'This Army unit is leaving tomorrow and I am going with them. We are being replaced by Military Government units. They will arrive tomorrow, take over from us and will be billeted in the *Gasthaus.*'

123

She told me its name but I have forgotten it.

'Call there – say – the day after tomorrow. They will be looking for interpreters and they do not like to employ Germans so you should be all right,' she advised.

Two days later, accompanied by Alice, as I was apprehensive of going into any military unit on my own having had more than enough of uniforms, we went to the *Gasthaus*.

An English soldier stood on guard at the entrance.

'Is this the office of the Military Government?' I asked.

'Yes, it is,' he politely replied.

'Could I please speak to one of your officers?' I continued in faultless English.

'What's your business?' he said.

'I want a job as an interpreter.'

'Wait here.'

He went inside. A few minutes later he returned and beckoned us to follow. Even at midday the large room was gloomy. At the back there was a large open window, to the right a long bar and in front of us two long wooden tables with benches on either side. The tables and benches stretched the full length of the room. Two officers stood by one of the tables; one was young and fair, the other elderly and completely white haired. We sat down, the table between us.

It was the white-haired one who spoke to us.

'You want to work as an interpreter? You speak English?' he began.

'Yes, I do, I have had English lessons since I was a small child.' I replied.

'Are you German?'

'No, I come from Czechoslovakia.'

'Do you speak any other languages beside English?' he then asked.

'Yes, I am fluent in German, Hungarian, Slovak and Czech and I speak French to about the same level as English and I get by in Russian.'

The young officer burst out laughing. 'I don't believe it! How can anyone speak so many languages?'

He thought he had made a joke but I took it to be a perfectly valid question. The English sense of humour was, as yet, unknown to me.

'In my primary school the teaching language was German and I also went to the German High School, where the teaching language was also German, with French as a second language. I then went to a Gymnasium where we were taught in Slovak and Czech and my father is Hungarian.'

'And the Russian?' he ventured.

'We also learned Russian at school.'

'Where did you learn English?'

'My father has two cousins who live in England. I was supposed to come to boarding school in England in 1938 but things got difficult and then the war started.'

'How come you're in Bielefeld?'

'We were taken from Auschwitz to an armament factory in Lippstadt on the Ruhr last autumn. I worked first as a nurse but then they put me into the factory on night shifts. When the air raids became really bad the factory stopped working; there was no more iron. They took away the sick in wagons. We were then marched during the nights and hidden in the daytime. The Americans liberated us. I was ill and my friends got me into the hospital here. I am well now and can leave the hospital. I need work.'

'Don't you want to go home?' he said.

'No, I don't think that there will be anyone left to go home to.'

Without my noticing it, two other officers had come in

during our conversation. One had stood near the bar, the other had gone to the window and was leaning out.

He now turned round and said to the one near the bar, 'If you don't mind, I'll take her on.'

That is how I met Bert - Capt (QM) H. Knill.

They all now came to the table and introduced themselves. The one near the bar was Lt. Col. Berry-Steege, the commanding officer; the fair one Lieutenant Hector Purver, the transport officer; the white haired one Capt. George Cann, the security officer and Bert was the quartermaster and second-in-command.

'We are leaving here tomorrow. Where do we pick you up?'

'I thought you were stationed here,' I said, astonished.

'No, we are only travelling through; we are the 1027 Military Government Detachment and we will be stationed in Büren. Is it important for you to be here?'

'No, there is no reason why I should be here rather than anywhere else. I am staying at the hospital. At what time will you come for me?'

'Between ten and eleven.'

Turning to Alice, he added, 'Do you also want a job?'

I translated for her and she asked me to tell them that she did not speak English or German, was waiting to go back to the camp and then home to Hungary.

We walked back to the hospital. I told my nun that I had got a job with the British Army and that they would fetch me in the morning. There was a flurry among them. How could I go with nothing, just the clothes I had made and stood up in?

They found a small grey fibreboard suitcase about the size of a shopping bag, it had seen better days. They had already given me a toothbrush and some rather rough soap. To this was added a piece of towel and a rosary. I put my spare blouse and knickers in the case. Next morning, folding my coat over my arm and suitcase in hand, I stood on the hospital steps waiting to be collected.

A jeep rolled up with Lt. Purver and his driver. They got out.

'Where is your luggage?' he asked.

'This is it,' I replied, holding up my small suitcase.

BY THE TIME WE arrived in Büren, at the big house with the large garden that had belonged to the *Landrat*, the provincial governor, the courtyard was a hive of activity. Lorries were being unloaded; soldiers were carrying in tables, desks, chairs, typewriters, camp beds, rolls of bedding, kit bags – everything, including the kitchen sink. Bert (Captain H.) was presiding over the organised chaos. We got out of the Jeep and he came over.

He said to Hector Purver, 'Your room has been allocated and your kit has been unloaded, your batman is unpacking.'

He turned to me and added, 'We'll have to find a billet for you, because this is a military set-up and civilians cannot live here. Also, you are a girl and that could cause problems. I have set aside a small room for your meals and use when you are off-duty. For tonight I have had a camp-bed put there for you. Where is your luggage?'

I picked up my case.

'Hmmm … you travel light,' he observed. 'We'll fit you out tomorrow with a uniform and find you a billet. But, first of all, come with me to the kitchen. There is a German cook and we have brought an army cook with us and unless we do something quickly they will start another war.'

It was fortunate that soldiers in the British Army came in all shapes and sizes and although I found out later that there was also a female element, the uniforms here were only for one sex, male. I was fitted out with two sets of battledress, a greatcoat, belt and two shirts. The latter were rather scratchy; I thought I would prefer my white blouses and fortunately, I also had my home-made knickers. The Army drawers supplied were not even Y-fronted but loose and baggy and just would not have been suitable. All uniformed personnel wore shoulder flashes to identify them; ours said 1027 Mil Gov Det and, as instructed, I sewed a set of these to the top of the sleeves of the battledress. Officially, I was not entitled to wear them but it was thought that it would confuse not only Army personnel but also civilians, if I was not suitably 'labelled'. After all, there were other British troops stationed locally, besides the Military Government outfit and they had been billeted with the German population.

I was paid in 'script', occupational currency, which could be used in German shops. Everything was rationed. I got a 'chitty' from the office so that I could buy some shoes. I was glad of the British Army uniform but had drawn the line on army boots. I purchased two pairs of shoes, one lace-up brown and black pumps with high heels. I also bought three small pieces of felt in red, white and blue and made the Czechoslovak emblem out of them to put on my sleeves.

Bert thought it all looked too plain, very much like an 'Other Rank' and that I ought to look more like an officer. Officers were respected by Other Ranks and by the Germans. He produced a gold-coloured officer's braided cord and a whistle to be attached to my left shoulder strap, which he thought could also be useful in emergencies.

The next day I was told that a suitable lodging had been found for me. We drove into the residential area of Büren and stopped in front of No 2, the Luftgarten. The house belonged to a dressmaker and her family, her husband was in the army. She had two daughters and was quite happy to have me billeted on her rather than soldiers. I got a large sunny room on the first floor and settled in.

In the mornings, I walked up from the Luftgarten to the office and, before going to my desk, I went into the kitchen for a cup of coffee and a bread roll and inspected with the cook the provisions which had been brought in. We were joined by Capt. H and discussed what the menu for the day should be. Three cooked meals were the order of the day, obviously.

Before long Cookie, the German cook, developed a sign language of her own to indicate fish, pork, lamb or venison. Beef, though, beat her, she didn't think that pretending to have horns would give the right impression. She only cooked for the officers and me. The two kitchen maids who assisted her also cleaned the mess rooms. The Officers' quarters were serviced by the batmen, who were also supposed to serve at table; but the girls gradually took that role over. The officers preferred to be served by the girls but if high-ups came, or on formal occasions, the batmen were reinstated.

The biggest problem in respect of food was the huge difference between the English and German style of cooking. Cookie was an excellent cook of the German school. It was incomprehensible to her that vegetables should be presented 'naked', that is, without dressing or a sauce which was usual for *Gemuse* in Germany. Plain, overcooked cabbage, which was then a normal part of English meals, was something she found quite unpalatable. I personally agreed with her. But still, if that was what the officers wanted, that was what they got.

A lot of food came in tins; corned beef and Spam were mainstays and Cookie soon had a whole repertoire of fried, baked, hashed variations on this theme. She found it incomprehensible that plain, sliced cold bully beef was really preferred.

The Woman Without A Number

One item supplied on a regular basis which defeated her was pilchards in tomato sauce. It was meant to be an alternative breakfast item, on toast. Nobody liked it so our store of pilchards in tomato sauce got bigger and bigger and I have no idea how, or if, they were ever used. Before long we all had dogs as pets, even me but they did not like pilchards either, nor did the house cat.

We also got, at least twice a week, fresh meat. In the German way this was always well done and in a sauce of some kind, rather than with gravy. I was used to it but not the British officers. One of the officers came back from leave with some Oxo cubes and a jar of mint sauce. The latter, he told me, was not to be used until we had some lamb and then it should be served, the Oxo was to make gravy. Juice, or rather jus was something I knew, but thick gravy?

As luck would have it, it was not long before we received lamb – or rather mutton, which was to be roasted for dinner. The big day for the mint sauce had arrived. The jar contained green gunk, which smelled and tasted evil. I asked Bert, and he said that it had to be diluted with vinegar. I passed this information on to Cookie.

About half an hour later Cookie was on the phone to me: could I please come to the kitchen. She had spooned some of the gunk into a cup and added some vinegar to it.

I tasted it. She tasted it. We looked at each other, shook our heads and spat it out. No, it was just not possible to serve something like this with the mutton. It was just too horrible. There must have been some mistake. Cookie and I conferred. Maybe this was meant to be some sort of flavouring for a sauce? There were no clues on the jar, no directions and no instructions. Cookie made a beautiful smooth béchamel sauce and seasoned it – not too liberally but delicately with the mint sauce, adding a little more vinegar and a soupcon of sugar to counteract the acidity. I tasted it and it was not bad at all. It should go well with the mutton. It was proudly presented in the sauce boat with the roast lamb.

'Where is the mint sauce?' someone asked. The waitress passed the sauce boat and the officers tasted it and fell about laughing.

This was not English mint sauce. The wonders of the English cuisine never ceased to amaze us, nor did the liking of the officers for what Cookie called 'nursery puddings', such as rice pudding, tapioca and semolina. Adults did not eat such food in Germany, tapioca was completely unknown and custard powder from the tin was an abomination, but relished at the mess table. But what Cookie produced from the occasional venison was sheer poetry.

WE WERE ALWAYS SHORT of fresh eggs and although it was quite possible to use the powdered variety for cooking, baking and even, if handled with extreme care, scrambling, nothing could beat a nice fried egg for breakfast. Bert had a brainwave.

At the bottom of our very large garden was a shed. It should not be difficult to convert that into a henhouse and to construct a run with the dannet (barbed) wire netting, of which the army seemed to have unlimited supplies. Two of the handier Other Ranks were instructed to make a home fit for birds.

A highly illegal barter, involving chocolates and coffee (the Germans were not keen on tea) resulted in six lovely hens inspecting their new domicile a couple of days later. They were supposed to be layers, but lay they did not. One of the Other Ranks was a country lad and offered the opinion that, 'Hens won't lay without a cock.'

So a cockerel joined them and ensured that everybody

woke up very early. He was not popular but the desired result was achieved, we had fresh eggs for breakfast.

The success of this foray into animal husbandry caused Bert to have more ambitious plans. One day, at dinner, he said: 'What are we going to eat at Christmas? There won't be any turkeys here – wouldn't it make sense to fatten up a couple of geese? We've got all that grass at the back and they wouldn't cost anything to keep.'

Bert, an old army hand, had incredible and innovative ideas about living off the land. The proposal was greeted with enthusiasm – after all the hens were a success. One of the Other Ranks was now nominated in charge of feathered animals, with which he seemed to have more of affinity than the combustion engine. Another enclosure was constructed but this one was moveable so that the geese could have continuous access to fresh grass – nobody had thought that there would also be a mess to clean up – and to include the small ornamental pond.

Three young geese arrived and one of them must have been a gander. Two geese went a-laying and then one of them went broody. The goslings hatched but the weather was rainy and cold, although it was still summer. Bert, who had a very soft streak with regard to animals, got concerned about the newly born catching cold and dying. The Other Rank in charge of feathered animals was ordered to gather up the goslings, Cookie was told to put the oven on its lowest setting and they were put on a large baking tray on the open door of the oven in a sort of improvised hatchery. Mother goose was none too happy about it but when, a couple of days later, six fluffy goslings made their appearance in her compound, she was quite willing to accept them as her own and paraded them proudly.

However, one gosling would not have anything to do with her mother. At a critical stage of her development she must have caught sight of Bert and decided that he was her mother and she followed him everywhere. If she could not get into the office, she sat outside the door, cheeping miserably and leaving puddles and worse. It did not matter how often she was put back with the other geese – as far as she was concerned they were strangers and she would not have anything to do with them. She wanted Bert and no one else would do.

One of the officers suggested killing her but he was nearly lynched for the suggestion. So she became a guardian house goose and was eventually house trained, except when she got too excited, which unfortunately happened quite frequently.

We did have roast goose for Christmas although by the time it came to kill the birds nobody was willing to do it and certainly not the Other Rank in charge of the feathered animals. In the end, the Other Ranks were told to hold a lottery, the winner had to kill the geese but would get a bottle of whisky.

ALTHOUGH, OFFICIALLY, WE COULD only keep three of the Mercedes cars that had been requisitioned from the Germans - beside the primitive Volkswagen's with removable canvas seats with which we were issued - it was decided that, to make certain that we kept those which were in the best running order, they had to be tested. Those we were not retaining were to be sent on to the Military Headquarters but having only three cars meant that not every officer had one. A devious scheme was adopted which had its origin in the fact that, by chance, we found two pairs of identical vehicles. Obviously, each car had a different registration number but otherwise they were completely the same.

The Woman Without A Number

For each car that we could hold legally we, therefore, now had a 'shadow' one, once identical number plates were put on. This was very useful because the cars frequently needed repairing. To complete the scam, the mileage clocks were also synchronised, identical log books were fabricated and the real, master log kept under lock and key and used when petrol had to be drawn at the military depot. Those using the cars were told to ensure that the two were never in the same area at the same time.

I learned to drive in one of the 'shadow' cars. In order to drive at all I needed a temporary driving licence and that was not something the Army or Military Government could provide. Bert and I went to the German licensing office and asked them to provide me with a provisional one. Neither of us had any idea under what condition the German authorities issued them and we soon found that it was a bureaucratic minefield. The official in charge explained that, in order to get a licence I had to take a long course of instruction at an accredited driving school and, since there was no petrol available for this, no such courses had been run in the recent past nor were they likely to in the near future. And driving schools had closed down as their instructors had gone into the army so she could not possibly issue me with a licence.

Eventually she responded to the authority of a uniform and a bribe of a pound of coffee and issued me with a temporary licence on which were typed the words: 'Issued on instruction of the Military Government.' I had my licence and she had covered herself.

Bert took me out to teach me. He drove until we got out of town, then we changed places and within five minutes he was fast asleep.

I stopped the car – he woke up and asked: 'Why did you stop?'

'You are supposed to teach me to drive,' I said. 'How can I learn if you fall asleep as soon as I start?'

'It just shows how confident I am in your driving,' he countered.

'But I can't drive!' I said in exasperation.

'You did just then.'

It was hopeless. In the end I asked one of our sergeants to let me go with him and the fifteen cwt truck when he went to collect rations and to explain to me what the various knobs, levers and pedals did. The problem was that the truck needed double de-clutching on all gears; the Mercedes only needed that for the first and second ones. An Opel - another car we had 'acquired' - needed double de-clutching like the truck, so that was the car I eventually drove. But I never learned to cope with its habit of jumping sideways.

In spite of Bert falling asleep every time I drove, I did become a competent driver.

Drinking and driving were not discouraged; on the contrary, people often drank to give them courage to drive! I did not, because I soon found that my drinking capacity was strictly limited to two, after which I was literally sick.

During the day I either worked in the office interpreting and translating and gradually acting as staff officer to Bert, or accompanying him or one of the other officers to interpret for them although I was not the only interpreter.

Col. Steege, the Commanding Officer, had been, so I understood, associated with MI5 and actually spoke immaculate German as I found out later. He unearthed from somewhere a German couple, Herr and Frau Muller who were his interpreters despite him not needing them. We also employed two female German interpreters once the non-fraternisation rule was relaxed, one of whom became firmly attached to Hector – in more ways than one; but all officers called on me when other languages were required.

The Woman Without A Number

Before long there was an Officers' Club in Lippspringe, where my presence became much sought after as, except for a couple of NAAFI officers, females with whom the officers were allowed to associate were few on the ground. Once a week, in accordance with tradition, the mess had 'Ladies Night', to which I was the only lady invited. The difficulty was what to wear. Battledress was okay for work but not mess nights. I turned to the dressmaker in whose house I lived. She said that she would make any dress I wished, but material was a different matter.

As luck would have it, a local inhabitant with a grudge leaked the information that in a certain house nearby there was a walled-up room full of goodies. Capt. Cann and a detachment of Other Ranks, accompanied by Bert and I, entered the house. It was searched thoroughly, inside and out. Before long it became obvious that the external and internal dimensions did not tally. There was also a curtained window, visible from the outside, which could not be accounted for. The owners, in fear and trembling, pleaded ignorance. I explained to them that the hiding of goods which had been rationed during the Reich was a civil offence which would be dealt with by the German authorities according to their laws. That resulted in floods of tears – evidently it was a capital offence. I had thought that all that would happen was that whatever was found would be confiscated and they would be fined. I assured them that there was no chance of them being hanged.

In the meantime, the wall in question, in front of which stood tall cupboards, was being tapped high and low, but proved to be solid. Sledgehammers were brought and a trial hole made. When it was large enough for an arm to go through, a torch was shone in and it was seen that the whole space was filled with racking. George Cann told me to ask the owner now very sternly:

'What have you been hiding there?'

'It is only stuff,' she ventured.

'What do you mean, stuff?' I continued.

'Stuff for making clothes and curtains and such like' they said.

'Nothing else?' I queried.

I told George what the owner had said.

'In that case we need the German authorities here, because it is really not a matter within our jurisdiction' he reflected.

I was sent with a jeep and driver to them and told to return with someone who was in charge of rationing. A rotund woman with steel spectacles and curly grey hair, carrying a large notebook came with me. On the way I told her what we appeared to have found.

She nodded: 'We always thought that they had not given up all their stock, but could not find out where they had hidden it. Did you see what was there?' she asked.

'I only saw racks full of rolls of fabric through a hole' I told her. 'The British would not enlarge it until someone was there who could take it over.'

'We shall be very pleased with whatever there is' she said.

When we got back Fraulein W. looked through the hole and threw up her arms in disbelief. 'This is more than we have had in years' she noted.

The soldiers set to with sledge hammers creating lots of dust and Fraulein W., no lightweight, had to be restrained from crawling into the hole until it was large enough to allow her to get through with ease.

It was an Aladdin's cave. Every kind of material in all the colour of the rainbow was there; velvets, silks, brocades, satins, cotton and linen.

Fraulein W. turned to me, 'We shall have to take stock of

all that is here. We will measure the quantity on each roll and seal it in front of witnesses. But we can't do that until tomorrow. Can you ask the Officer to put a guard here until we get here in the morning?'

I translated for George Cann and Bert.

Bert took me aside.

'Go back to your billet and get a pair of scissors' he whispered. 'Cut off what you need so that you have some decent clothes.'

I was modest, not at all greedy – although there was enough temptation there. I snipped away two lengths of fabric for evening dresses, one of black satin and one of taupe cloque, some dark blue flannel for a dressing gown and navy blue linen for two skirts and jackets. And I also found and took a whole roll of tracing paper because I knew, but doubted whether anyone else did, that if you boiled it all the dressing came off and you were left with the finest cotton lawn. From that could be made blouses and underwear.

Now I would be fit to face any occasion.

BÜREN WAS IN THE middle of a heavily forested area. The Germans had not been allowed to shoot in the preceding years and the countryside was overrun with wild boar and deer. Fields had been devastated by them and the forestry manager of the local authority called and asked whether it would be possible to arrange for some animals to be culled.

So started the season of shooting parties. Guided by the forestry officials, groups of officers went hunting at night. Although food and drink was taken along, any serious drinking reduced the chances of a successful venture.

Most of the meat went straight to the German authorities for distribution; the odd piece of venison made a welcome change to our diet. I sometimes accompanied them but did not find much enjoyment in the activity. Sitting for hours quietly in a hide and getting colder and colder was not my idea of fun.

On one occasion, when I was with Bert, we had followed the tracks of some wild boar. He imagined he saw one in the undergrowth and, leaning against the trunk of a tree to improve his aim, put his foot on what he thought was the bole. As it sunk in, a squealing piglet ran off followed by the rest of the family including a sizeable boar, which Bert shot successfully. It was a hair-raising experience getting so near to those animals: they could be very vicious indeed.

Bert went stag hunting only once, for roe deer, the smallest of the breed with a most beautiful speckled coat. Thinking he had shot one cleanly, when he got up to it, the animal was still alive and looked up at him. It was quickly despatched but Bert never went shooting again. Some big stags were bagged and the food supply of the German population increased significantly. Hector Purver took a credible pair of antlers back to the UK as proof of his own hunting prowess.

When Bert came back to England in 1947, he found out that the German authorities had charged the Military Government for every animal shot, in spite of them having been eaten by the Germans. I learned fly-fishing and angled for trout and grayling. The British Government were also billed for all the fish I caught!

10

*

Bert

When I saw Bert for the first time he appeared to me a tall, well-built, middle-aged man, with mousy hair, tending towards corpulence. As I got to know him, working beside him day by day, I saw his innate kindness, realised his wicked sense of humour and found the straight-faced way he had of telling bare-faced lies intriguing. One could never know whether he was telling the truth or not. He was the only person I ever knew who could be absolutely convincing in whatever he said. Even when you got to know him really well, you were left in complete confusion as to whether to believe him.

The English sense of humour was new to me. It appealed to me and I found over the years that I became quite adept at it myself, but then I liked to play with words. The habit of understatement was more difficult to come to terms with. From this distance of time it is difficult for me to sort out what I found about Bert then and what I got to know later.

He was born in 1899, the second of seven children; his father Thomas Knill was still alive, his mother, Emma

Underwood, had died some years ago. Thomas's father had been a brightsmith and a Freeman of the City of Bristol. Bert was the black sheep of the family, always getting into trouble and leaving school when aged twelve. By the time he was fourteen, he had been, among other things, a lather boy in a men's barber shop and a rivet boy in a shipyard.

When the First World War broke out he was fifteen and wanted to follow his older brother Alfred into the Army. He enlisted twice while under age and was bailed out by his parents, who then told him that if he tried again he would have to stay. Enough was enough – and he did.

So, when he was sixteen he enlisted in the Gloucestershire Regiment and found himself, after initial training, in the trenches and in the battle of Ypres. He spoke little of his experiences, but they must have been horrendous. Eventually he volunteered to be a stretcher-bearer, was gassed and hospitalised and saw his best friend blown to pieces while standing next to him.

There was little employment after the wars so he became a Regular Soldier. He served in the Duke of Cornwall's Light Infantry and rose to the rank of Regimental Sergeant Major. I don't think there was a part of the British Empire where he had not served.

In 1923, the year in which I was born, he married Winifred Downey, a nurse at the Bodmin Psychiatric Hospital – or Lunatic Asylum, as it was then called. In 1929 they adopted Peter David and in 1939 their son, Stuart Francis was born. By June 1939, Bert had completed his twenty-two years' service and was about to retire. He was to be a teacher of physical education at Truro Grammar School. At the same time he also joined the Territorial Army as Lieutenant Quartermaster, went to camp with them in the summer and found himself, within weeks, back in the Regular Army as the Second World War broke out.

The Woman Without A Number

Shortly afterwards, Winifred was diagnosed with breast cancer. She was operated on in May 1944, but her condition deteriorated rapidly. Bert's regiment was involved in the D-Day landing, but he was pulled out and sent back to Cornwall to sort out who was going to look after the children while his wife was in hospital and dying.

Bert came to Germany eventually with the Military Government in April 1945, but went back several times on compassionate leave until Win died in October 1945. Her wishes for her children were that Peter David should leave Truro Grammar School, although he was a brilliant student and be placed in the Army Apprentice School at Arborfield. He was to train as armourer. It seemed to be what he also wanted – the thought that he could have boarded at school was never considered. The Army would provide safety for him. Only on the journey to his final interview was he told that he had been adopted but not the circumstances nor the name of his birth parents. He needed to know this because it was on his birth certificate, which he had not seen before. At that time people were not aware – or concerned – about the trauma such a late disclosure could cause. Many years later Bert told me the circumstances of Peter's birth and who his parents were; I do not know, even now, whether Peter was ever told.

Stuart was only six when his mother died and he had spent the last two years being sent from one member of Win's family to another around Cornwall, never staying long, nor fitting in anywhere. Win did not think that her own family were the right people to bring him up and decided that he should go and live in Bert's home town, Bristol, with Bert's sister Doll and her husband Will, who had two little girls of nearly the same age. Bert would have preferred it if Stuart had gone to live with his godparents, Bert's brother Frank and Connie, who was a teacher, but the wishes of a dying woman are to be respected.

While Win was still alive I had become Bert's friend; he could talk to me about Win, about the children, his family and his life. I suppose, in a way, he provided for me the support my father had given me, who could, and would, talk to me at length while we went walking. I don't know whether Bert ever looked at me as the daughter he never had. He was a man's man, not a womaniser, like many of the others and I felt safe with him. After Win died he seemed to look to me more for support, not just as a listener and our companionship deepened.

I can't remember the actual moment when we realised that we had become more than friends, that we had developed a close understanding of each other, that we needed each other. That lay some time ahead, probably when he was posted as Magistrate to Paderborn, in the spring of 1946.

BEFORE THE WINTER OF 1945, many of the Displaced Persons had been repatriated. One of my cousins, Iby Foldes, uncle Imre's eldest daughter, had been in the Lippstadt camp with me. When she returned to Bratislava she found her father and her sister but neither her husband nor her mother had survived. She also heard that my mother had come back from the camp as well as my brother and another cousin from Hungary, where they had been hidden in the Swedish embassy but that there was no trace of me. She could only tell mother that she had been in the camp with me, that I had nursed her through typhoid, but that during the march I had become ill and had been taken to hospital.

It was usually mid-morning when the mail truck came back from headquarters and there was a letter for me; I could not believe it. The name and address of the sender on the back of the air-mail envelope meant nothing to me. I did not even know of the existence of the Czech Army in the UK, nor who was the officer who was writing to me. I opened the letter.

It said that a letter from an Irena Kaufmannova was enclosed, who had been informed by the International Red Cross that her daughter Ibolya was alive and working for the British in Germany. Was I that person? If so – here was my mother's letter.

I was thunderstruck. I had not anticipated that anybody from my family would be alive. Mother wrote that my father had not returned from Auschwitz, that there was no trace of Marton nor of Gaspar, but would I please come home.

I do not want to appear a cold-blooded person. I was immensely glad that my mother and brother had survived but I had left home more than three years ago, in the spring of 1942. I had gone through so many trials on my own that I felt detached from my family and could not envisage life back in Bratislava. Gaspar was dead – probably my whole generation had disappeared – what was there to go home for? What would I do there? After a lot of thinking I wrote to my mother that I was working, happy in my job and would probably come back one day, but not yet.

I had a reply, not from my mother, but from my cousin twice removed, Hugo. He wrote that mother missed me, that she was trying to re-establish the business, that Tomy was too young and should really continue his education and that my place was at home. He said that so few people had returned that it was a lonesome place. He himself had found somebody and was now married.

The only thing that would have made me leave straight away was if Hugo had written that he was waiting for me to return. I had always had a soft spot for him. But with Gaspar dead and Hugo married, where was I to start the hunt for a suitable husband? Would I ever find one there? Was I going to live the rest of my life in an environment where every house, every street, would remind me of friends and family I had lost? Where my mainstay, my father, was no longer there?

I could not cope with that. I was not strong enough. I wrote back in the same strain as I had to mother. Maybe one day but not yet.

BERT HAD ALWAYS LIKED a drink and all the officers drank heavily. The allocation of whisky, gin and brandy could be augmented with locally purchased 'Doppelkorn', a raw grain-based spirit which was only palatable when topped up with evaporated milk, and 'Steinhager' a gin-type alcohol which had to be diluted with fruit juice. German wine was plentiful and there was also an allocation of champagne in the Officers' rations.

Bert, being second in command and quartermaster, was responsible for indenting, receiving and distributing the monthly allocation of spirits to the individuals and for the Mess. In his room there was a locked cupboard in which surpluses and acquisitions were kept to be distributed and used judiciously.

After Bert came back from Win's funeral his drinking started to cause me concern. Previously, it had been restricted to the evenings but now the one-bottle-a-week man became a one bottle-a-day man who was frequently late in the morning and fell asleep after lunch in the Mess. Berry-Steege, who had been the commanding officer and knew Bert well, was no longer with us and I tried, as best as I could, to cover for Bert and make excuses for his frequent indisposition. The younger officers did not seem to realise the seriousness of the situation and just laughed it off as 'one of Bert's funny ways'.

The Woman Without A Number

When, one morning he had not appeared in the office by ten and we started work at 8.30, I phoned up to the kitchen to find out whether they knew where Captain Knill was.

A worried Cookie answered the phone:

'Fraulein Kaufmann, he has not had his breakfast, the batman could not get into his room, so he has not had his morning cup of tea either. He does not answer when we knock on the door. I was just going to phone you – what should we do? I have no idea what to cook for dinner.'

I went upstairs and knocked on Bert's door. No reply. I knocked again.

'Bert, it's me, Let me in,' I said.

'Leave me alone.'

'Bert, it's eleven o'clock. You are supposed to preside at the Court at two. Please, you have to get up.'

'I can't get up,' he countered.

'Why not?'

'Is anybody else with you?'

'No, I am alone,' I assured him.

'OK. I'll unlock the door. But you must count to ten before you come in and then lock the door behind you.'

Bert unlocked the door. I counted to ten. Went in, turned round and re-locked the door. Bert was in bed.

'Why are you in bed? Are you ill?' I asked.

'No, I am not ill, but I cannot get up,' he responded.

'Why ever not?'

'Look in my wardrobe.'

Where previously there had been rows of uniforms; battle dress, service dress, cotton and silk shirts, there was nothing.

'Look in the drawers.'

Where before had been underwear and socks there was nothing. I turned to Bert.

'What has happened? Where are your clothes?' I queried.

'I can't quite remember. We drank a lot and played strip poker. I must have lost all my clothes. I can't get up because I have nothing to put on.'

He was stark naked in bed. There was not a single item of clothing there, not even shoes.

'I'll see what I can do,' I told him. 'I'll ask the others.'

'I am mortified,' he confided.

That was most unusual coming from Bert. I went down into the offices and confronted each of the officers. They all thought it had been a great lark that Bert had lost his clothes fair and square and it was just too bad that he would have to come to the office wrapped in a sheet. They relented eventually and returned some, but not all, of his wardrobe.

By lunchtime a more sober and subdued Bert appeared. I was interpreting for him in court that day. When the session was over and we were walking back to the office, I asked him whether the experience had taught him anything – hoping he would say that he would watch his drink consumption. Instead he commented, 'I am not likely to play strip poker with those buggers again.'

BERT ACTED AS MAGISTRATE in Büren. Most of the cases that came before him concerned thefts of a particular type. We were in a semi-rural area and although rationing was strict, there were ways of obtaining food. Most households had hens in their backyards, grew vegetables and potatoes and stored them in the cellars. That was not an option open to people living in towns. Many of them travelled to the country in the hope of buying or acquiring food, even to the extent of raiding the clumps of roots in the fields. They were frequently caught and brought before the court but were starving and desperate people; to sentence them seemed an anachronism to Bert.

The Woman Without A Number

When they were brought into court by the police, the contrast between the well-fed constabulary and these poor wretches was painful to see. They protested that they could not get their rations in town, that their wives and children were starving and that they were at their wits' end what to do. They had hitch-hiked down and had no idea how they were going to get back home.

'We are not criminals, Sir, but we are desperate,' they pleaded.

Bert asked the prosecutor. 'What happens if I sentence them according to the law?

He replied, 'They are locked up.'

'Do they get fed in prison?'

'Of course, Sir, we would not let them starve. They'll have two cooked meals a day, as well as bread for breakfast.'

'What is the maximum sentence?' asked Bert.

'In this case, only twenty-one days.'

'Good,' said Bert, 'I sentence them each to twenty-one days.' Turning to the police officer he added, 'Make certain that they are properly fed.'

He then turned to the accused. 'It's not my place to say so – but if there is a next time, bring your wives and families, too.'

The next day Bert sent me down to the city jail with money to pay for the wretches to travel home by rail.

It might not have been justice 'by the book', but it was certainly 'justice by the heart'. However, it was not particularly popular with the locals who thought that it would encourage more thieves to come from the towns.

Bert's big-heartedness and common sense endeared him to the Germans eventually and when they heard he had been moved to preside at the District Court at Paderborn, lots of little gifts, with no names attached, arrived at the office.

But by this time it was spring 1946.

IN THE CONTINENTAL WAY, I had been used to the main celebration of Christmas being on Christmas Eve, when presents were exchanged. I had decided that, so as not to show favouritism, I would make presents for all the officers. By now, some of the original ones had been demobbed and replaced by Short Service Officers and one or two of them had leave to go to the UK for Christmas. From that roll of tracing fabric which had become fine lawn I cut out handkerchiefs – three for each officer, hemstitched them and embroidered their initials in one corner. A lot of time and effort went into it.

A couple of days before Christmas a big tree arrived and was set up in the mess room. Decorations were mainly paper chains; one of the officers had thoughtfully brought them back from his trip home and also some tinsel and we managed to obtain small candles and candle holders. The Army also provided some paper chains and paper lanterns and it all looked very festive.

When I came up to the Officers' Mess for dinner on Christmas Eve, I put my little parcels of presents under the tree. I wish I had had a camera to take a picture of the officers' sheepish faces. They had all been punishing the bottle and Christmas Eve for them was nothing special and presents were unexpected. Army tradition decreed that, in the true spirit of the Roman Saturnalia, on Christmas Day the Other Ranks feasted in the Officers' Mess and were waited on by the Officers. I was told to absent myself; things could get out of hand. We would have our Christmas meal – roast goose – in the evening.

Cookie got very flustered as Christmas approached. It was all so different, not only in respect of the food. She was used to cooking for eight or nine but now had to conjure a feast for twenty, to be followed on the same day by another one in the evening. Not much of a Christmas for her and her girls – but somehow nobody thought about that.

After my disappointment of Christmas Eve, there was not much for me to do on Christmas Day in the morning. I offered to come and help Cookie, who accepted my offer with alacrity. The Other Ranks had roast pork, followed by Christmas pudding. That was another mystery for Cookie and me but we just did what it said on the package although neither of us could understand how anybody could eat that black heavy stuff which had to be steamed for hours, then set alight and served with custard. The officers were kept busy, serving food and drink. On the insistence of the Other Rank in charge of farm animals, the house-trained goose had to join them and have her own seat at table. I was told that the moment she saw Bert she again followed him around, as usual, getting under everybody's feet and misbehaving on the carpet. However, it all added to the general merriment. By the time we sat down to dinner in the evening, the Other Ranks were sleeping it off and the carpet had been cleaned.

And, I did get some presents.

TIME PASSED, THE WEATHER improved and Bert and I became friends. I suggested to Bert that we explore the countryside. This suggestion was welcomed and the excursions were not restricted to the two of us. We went to the Mohne Damm, the Opera at Bielefeld, the theatre and one or more of the officers usually came with us.

The Officers' Club at Bad Lippspringe had been the Kursahl – the equivalent to the Pump Room at Bath. There was a large entrance lobby, a bar with lots of comfortable seating, a rostrum for a band and a central area for dancing, surmounted by a cupola, the middle glass section of which could be opened to let in fresh air and allow us to see the stars above the smoke we generated. In those days everybody smoked heavily.

Then there was also the dining room. Waiters and other staff were German but food supplies came mainly from the NAAFI and female NAAFI officers were also members. I could go as a guest. That was where I got introduced to the drink Black Velvet, which has remained one of my favourite tipples.

It was time out of context – the war was over and we were young and alive. Effectively, rugby scrums took the place of dancing – after all, what could be done when there were at most three females among a hundred officers? There were no rugby balls – a cushion had to take its place. An open window served as goal and one of the waiters was deputed to stand outside and retrieve the ball, run round, bring it in and throw it into the scrum.

Normally, this was exclusively male territory; ladies could come on Saturday nights and behaviour was usually slightly more restrained when we were there. There were a few occasions that became legend. On one, bets were laid on how high the glass dome was. Estimates varied greatly and there did not seem to be a way to resolve the question.

One bright spark had the idea that, if they made a human pyramid in the centre of the floor and someone climbed up with a piece of string, held on to one end and let the other end down, it would be possible to measure this piece of string and then the winner could collect his winnings. No sooner said than done.

Usually, when things threatened to get riotous, the senior officers left the club and that is what happened at this juncture. As most of the officers remaining had by now drunk a fair amount, the pyramid kept on collapsing long before it reached the necessary height. There was much laughter but those who had placed bets did not think it funny. It was becoming a serious matter and the punters grew more and more determined to get the measure.

One of the waiters had been sent for a ball of string and he stood ready with it to hand on to the lucky, or rather plucky, chap who would scale the pyramid. The glass dome was opened a fraction, cold air and slight snow blew down but proved to be no deterrent. As the most senior officer present Bert Knill was elected – or elected himself - to reach for the top. He was a six-footer, a sportsman and no featherweight and certainly not the lightest or the slightest of men. He started to climb up the pyramid. It swayed but more and more officers came along to support the lowest tier. In Bert's trouser pocket was the ball of string. He reached the top, put his right arm over the edge of the opened glass dome, trying to steady himself while reaching into his pocket to get the string – and then promptly dropped it, which was hardly surprising due to his inherent clumsiness.

Those supporting him tried to catch the ball as it descended and, in their efforts to do so, the pyramid collapsed, leaving Bert up in the cupola, hanging on by his arm outside the glass. The snow was now coming down heavily. Bert shouted, 'Get that bloody pyramid back up again. I want to come down.' By now, though, everybody was helpless, either through drink or laughter. Several attempts at reconstructing the pyramid failed. Those watching laughed more and more as Bert got colder and colder, angrier and angrier and progressively started to sober up.

'Get a ladder, somebody!' he shouted.

It was brought but proved far too short as did the next one found. The suggestion was made that a blanket should be held by several officers and Bert should be encouraged to jump. He fiercely resisted this suggestion, saying – wisely - that he would not trust them to catch a cat in a blanket. 'I know you lot!' he said, exasperated. 'You are going to drop it just as I jump. I am not going to do this. Phone the fire brigade!'

They agreed, put their pride into their pockets and phoned for the German fire brigade.

In the meantime, just in case it took too long for them to come or Bert got so cold that he could no longer keep his tenuous grip on the edges of the cupola, all the cushions were taken off the chairs and settees and piled up in the middle of the floor.

The fire brigade came yet wanted to be paid up front for this rescue because there was no fire. All the money which had been collected for the bets on the height of the cupola went to pay the fire brigade, who brought Bert down safely. As to the height, if they had asked one of the waiters – in German – he could have told them.

ONCE VJ DAY WAS celebrated, the British soldiers started to return to the UK to be demobbed. The first ones to go were the Other Ranks who were replaced by German civilians. Before long we had German drivers and store men but a nucleus of soldiers remained to deal with confidential matters in the office. The first officer to go was Col. Steege, who was replaced by a short-service officer, or rather several, because none of them seemed to stay for longer than a couple of months. British police officers joined us as did British civil servants, some of whom were led a merry dance by the officers remaining, because they made no effort to fit in and were fish out of water. Bert was formally transferred to the Control Commission, Germany, who took over from the Military Government in January 1946.

The Woman Without A Number

It was soon noticed that civil servants caused paper work. They decreed that there should be a complete census of all German industrial and commercial undertakings, employing more than two persons, including the owner. These forms had sixteen pages and every part had to be completed, we received a lorry-load of them. Fortunately for the Germans they were in their native language but there was no English translation and the chap from the Ministry, who had joined us for this specific project, had no knowledge of German.

I was asked to translate the form and set up a sample paper in English. All well and good– but my knowledge of technical English was nil. We had one dictionary but that proved of little use. Every so often I came up against a word, an expression in German, for which I did not know the exact equivalent. Sometimes I thought that the dictionary definition would be right. That was how Wasserleitung became Aqueduct rather than 'water-laid-on'. I had never heard of 'water-laid-on'. It became a standing joke, 'Is the water hot in the aqueduct in the bathroom?'

I had by this time established friendly relations with Fraulein W. the chief local government operative and that smoothed the ways of officialdom. I phoned her and arranged a meeting between her, the ministry official and myself. I showed her the forms and told her that they had to be filled in by every undertaking. Forms caused no apprehension to her, being German she was used to them but when she saw these, she visibly blanched.

'Who is supposed to complete these?' she wondered.

'The people themselves,' I told her

'I do not think that this will work. Let me look at them….. They have to provide documents and plans?' she went on.

'Yes,' I confirmed.

'We do have a list of all undertakings,' she mused. 'I think it is best if we write to all of them, telling them to get the necessary information together and asking them to come into the office so that the form can be completed there and then they can sign it. Otherwise the forms will go back and forth to be amended and we'll never know when all have come in.'

I told the Ministry chap what Fraulein W. had said. He thought that it was a splendid idea especially as it would save him work. So it was agreed they should attend in alphabetical order and that queries would be sorted out straight away. Fraulein W. was to lend us three clerks to help complete the forms and it worked. I moved between the clerks, clearing up any queries and within a fortnight a lorry load of forms went back to where they had come from. We were told that we were the first unit that managed to complete them and the only one where there were no follow ups. The chap from the Ministry took the credit and was so puffed up about it that he was difficult to live with. But, having done his job so well, he was shortly recalled to London, which did not overly please him because he had come to like the fleshpots of occupied Germany very much indeed.

The next task with which I became involved was the setting up of local elections and the voting in of the Mayor. In spite of all the officers having had a three-week course on local government before they came to Germany, none of them had any practical knowledge of its workings, so a book about it was sent to us, along with lots more forms and directives. The Commanding Officer, now a Major Green, did not wish to have German interpreters with him when he visited the existing local council and was supposed to explain to them how democracy worked. I had borrowed the book and had read the directives. Interpreting for Major

The Woman Without A Number

Green, I explained how voting papers should be prepared, voting be conducted, votes counted and results announced. They all nodded – all this made sense. They asked, however, why this should be done, since there were only as many of them as there were places for counsellors. The idea that anybody could stand for election caused consternation.

It was explained to them that every person would first be vetted by the British – which included them. More consternation ensued. They protested that they were all anti-Nazis, had never had anything to do with the Nazi Party. How then had they come to power under Nazism I wondered? Still they protested their innocence. Major Green and I waited for the hubbub to subside. We explained that posters would be put up, notices would appear and that each proposed had to have twenty supporters for their candidacy to be valid. We told them that we would be available to answer questions, would be there for the counting of the votes but would take no part of any kind in the election. We were only here to advise them how to do it – but it was up to them to run it. They found that very surprising. They were used to being told not only what to do but also how to do it. It seemed very strange to them, they suspected a ruse and that the English were bound to favour some candidates over others.

During the next weeks while the process of the election was going on, I fielded innumerable questions, to all of which the answer was, 'You have to decide that yourself.' They did not like it.

'But what do you really want us to do?' they kept insisting.

They were very insistent. They were used to being ordered or at least given indications as to what the preferred course of action was so they felt completely at sea and at a loss.

156

It was difficult to sell democracy to people who could not understand that it meant freedom of choice. But worse was to come. The election over, it was time for the first sitting of the local council. Major Green and I attended. He stood up and I translated for him.

'Before you can carry out any business, you have to elect amongst you a spokesperson, a chairman, who will be your mayor for the next year. It can be any of you. On the sheet of paper in front of you put the name of the person you wish to be the chairman. The only one you cannot vote for is yourself. Fold the paper in four so no one can see who you have voted for. Miss Kaufmann (that was me) will collect the papers. You will then have coffee in the other room. We will call you back when we have counted the votes and have a result.'

I had already prepared a checklist of all those elected and now marked with a tick the votes; Major Green double checking. The outcome was a majority vote for one who, naturally, had already been cleared by MI5 as fit to stand. We called them back.

Major Green announced, 'Herr B... has been elected mayor by nine votes to six.'

Herr B stood up, red in face.

'No, I am not going to be Mayor. No, I am not!' he shouted.

'Why ever not? You have been elected!' Major Green replied.

'No, I have not been elected by everybody. If everybody does not choose me then I won't be Mayor.' He banged the table in front of him.

Major Green was very nearly speechless.

'But, but, this is democracy! In a democracy, the majority rules. Nobody else has received as many votes as you, so the majority wants you,' he declared.

The Woman Without A Number

'But not everybody!' More thumping on the table.

Old habits die hard and Major Green's simile, 'You can't say you won't play and then take the ball home with you,' was difficult to translate.

Eventually, Herr B did accept with ill grace. Democracy was going to have a tough time.

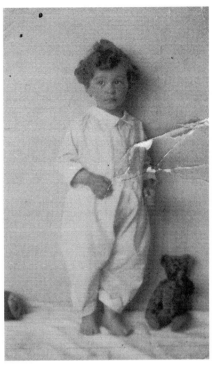

Clockwise - 1921: Engagement photo of my parents, Irene Elbogen, Beno Kaufmann;
1925: Iby, aged about 18 months; 1926: Bikinis had not yet been invented…;
1927: Iby, aged about 4 (I liked dogs, even then, even if they were stuffed)

Clockwise - 1929: In the garden of Palisady 51. Pictured from left, Grandma Elbogen, Iby, Mother with Tomy, aged 4 months, Grandfather Elbogen. In background, family members; 1928: Mother, Grandma and Iby; 1931: Iby and Tomy

Pictured from top -

1931: Karlsbad or Karlovy Vary. Mother, Iby, cousin Edith, Grandma, Tomy and Father;

1932: Primary school, Tedesco Herman Stiftung. Sixty in a class! Iby is third from right, top row;

1934: Our own car, a Model T Ford. Tomy is driving, cousin Gertie and I are in the back

Top left - 1937: Tomy and I - in the Austrian mode; *Above* -1938: Iby, the 15-year-old Beauty Queen;

Below - 1945: 1027 Military Government Detachment

Above - 1945: Kaunitz. Some of the 700 women liberated by American forces on 1 April. *Below* - 1945: Buren. Outside the Landrat office - 1027 Military Government Detachment - Iby, her dog, driver and clerks

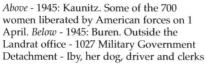

Clockwise - Various photographs of Bert and I.

1946: The day after our wedding – on 4 December;

1946: Major H. Knill;

1948: In the garden of 'Viview' (called that in view of the viaduct across the valley);

1947: At Birmingham Bull Ring

Above - 1940: Passport photo of my father

Left - 1949: Iby and Chris

Above: 1942: Marton Pollak, my cousin in Budapest

Right: 1950: Springtime

Above - 1975: Family memorial in cemetery, Bratislava (Mother had remarried. Imrich Foldes, my late father's cousin)

Left - 1960: At the Home Office Civil Defence School, Falfield

Above - May, 2010: At the site of the ruins of the brickyard at Székesfehervár
© Andy Boag

Above - 2003: Iby is awarded an MA in Theology and Religious Studies, University of Leeds, at York Minster

11

*

Married To England

Most of the military had now moved out of Büren and billeting had been discontinued. My landlady's husband had returned from the army and her dressmaking business was getting busier. She was nice about it but she really needed my room so I found a small flat at the other end of the town.

I now worked exclusively for the British Public Prosecutor, who had been seconded to the job from Britain. Bert, now in Paderborn, drove over on weekends and sometimes in the evening and we spent the time together in my sparsely furnished rooms or going out for drives; it was not an ideal situation. He phoned me often at the office but it was not a private line.

In the early summer of 1946 Bert asked me two things: would I be willing to move over to Paderborn if a suitable post could be found for me and – nearly in the same breath – he had no right to ask but would I marry him? There was nothing to hold me in Büren. I did miss Bert, I had not made close friends with any of the civil servants or the German staff. I said yes to the first question but asked him to wait for an answer to the second. After all, it was no more than six months since Win had died and we really needed to talk seriously about the implications.

Within a fortnight I was offered a job in the District Court at Paderborn, doing more or less what I had been doing in Büren except that this was a Higher Court and the cases which came before it were much more serious. Three officers were the judges and one of them was Bert. He had made friends with the other two, one a solicitor, the other an experienced police officer from Oxford. By now, I had been positively vetted by Special Branch.

Paderborn a biggish town, had been badly bombed and accommodation was at a premium. There was no question of my being billeted but a tiny room was found for me in a German house and I made arrangements to have my breakfast and evening meal with the family. I had also been issued with a German ration card which I handed over to them and also promised that there would be extras in the way of food, as and when I could get hold of it, as well as half a kilo of coffee beans a month. The latter clinched the deal, coffee beans were like gold dust.

On my first weekend there Bert and I went out for a drive – to talk. I explained my background, my circumstances, that I had been born Jewish, but had been through a form of baptism in 1942, but did not know how valid it was. He said this did not matter to him at all; his best friend in his early years had been Jewish – so what? He added that his handicaps - the difference in our ages and his two sons, who needed bringing up, were much greater. I told him that due to experiments in the camp it was unlikely that I could ever have children. He said he had two sons already and that was enough for any man. He advised that my life might not be a bed of roses because he did not know how his family would react but that he loved me and needed me. We agreed that Bert would submit an application for Permission to Marry, which he had to do as a regular officer, and that we would sort out the question of my religion; I told him how for me it was very important that all members of a family should have the same one. I had seen too many problems caused by religious differences in families.

A week or so later, Bert managed to contact the Padre at the Military Headquarters. He came over to see us and wanted to speak to me on my own. His concern was that I wanted a 'marriage of convenience' to get to England and that was the only reason for my 'conversion' and proposed marriage.

I can't remember the exact words I used but I told him that until my early teens I had not known that I was Jewish or what being Jewish meant and that, when I did, it had made me feel guilty and ashamed and that I resented it, although I could not work out why I felt this way. I added that I had had to leave my education, my home, my family and how Father Andreas had baptised me and given me an identity to help me through the turmoil of the next years.

How no God would answer prayers in Auschwitz, how I felt angry with a God who could be so thoughtless, so negligent of his Chosen people that I had no wish to be ever more associated with him.

'But there is really only one God,' he interjected.

'So where was he?' I questioned. 'What was he doing? If he existed he had turned his face away from the suffering. I cannot cope with such a God. Were we made to bear the cross and to call: Father, Father, why have you forsaken me? And get no answer?'

'Nor did Christ,' he reminded me.

'He did eventually,' I interjected. 'I do not want this God of wrath, of retribution. I am searching for, I need, a God of

161

Love, who will provide me with the one point of certainty in the world. Maybe I want the impossible. Maybe he does not exist.'

The Padre was silent.

'What would happen if the Army refused permission to marry?' he said.

'That is not the subject in question nor does it have a bearing on what I have told you,' I answered. 'If I am to marry Bert I feel that I have to be a bona fide Christian, of the same denomination as he is, because he has children and I would be their mother. It is just not feasible nor advantageous to have different religions in one household. Anyhow, what is my religion? According to Father Andreas I would be Catholic; according to the Nazis I was still Jewish. I have no certificate of baptism but then I have no identification document of any kind, except the one issued to me in the camp.' I continued, 'Even if I do not marry Bert I have no wish to return to Czechoslovakia. I have been told that I could emigrate to Australia, where I have relatives, or to Palestine where I have two cousins, but I have no desire to do so. My father's brother is in America, if he is still alive. I also have an aunt, Lady Chapman, in England and was on my way to England when Austria was occupied in 1938. Except for the two cousins in Palestine, none are Jewish, so why should I be? I do not wish to carry this burden nor to pass it on to any children I might have. But as a Padre should your concern not be more with spiritual matters?'

'One can't detach one from the other. I can see your reasoning, but need to know whether you accept the Christian Dogma,' he said solemnly.

'Father Andreas only asked me whether I believed in God and in good and evil,' I countered. 'I do. Are things so different in the Church of England? What else is there of importance?'

He gave me a booklet, told me to read it thoroughly and

162

to telephone him in a week's time. If I felt 'comfortable' [that was the word he used] with the contents, he would arrange for a combined baptism and confirmation.

'Then there won't be any question of where you belong,' he said.

'And if I am not comfortable with this?'

'Think about it carefully and pray – you will find the answer, one way or the other. In any case, contact me.'

There were one or two items I had doubts about. I asked Bert, he reassured me that this was not at all unusual, that one should not throw out the baby with the bath water, the Church of England could be very broad and whatever you wanted it to be. It was an unorthodox theological point of view. I phoned the Padre. He borrowed a German Protestant church; Bert and his friend, the Oxford Police Officer, were my sponsors. I was formally baptised and confirmed into the faith of the Church of England and issued with two certificates. Heaven knows where they are now.

THE ARMY REFUSED TO give Bert permission to marry me. He was certain, being experienced in the way of their procedures, that there would be more than one way to get round it. When his application to marry me was returned, stamped 'Not Approved', he hit the roof. It was the first time I saw him lose his cool – and he was formidable. I was with him when he opened the envelope.

He lifted the receiver and bellowed into it, 'Get me … at HQ and make it quick.' It was not long before the call came through.

He turned to me and said matter-of-factly, 'You better get out. You may not want to hear this.'

I did but I think everybody could hear what Bert had to tell the officer at the other end:

'It's bad enough for an officer after twenty-seven years' service having to ask permission to marry,' he began. 'Okay, they are the rules. But what rules and regulations tell you that I cannot marry who I choose?'

We could imagine the replies on the other end but it was a one-way conversation.

'Unsuitable? What are you talking about?' he went on.

'No, it damn well is not a marriage of convenience, except for me.'

'Her background? How dare you! A darn sight better than mine or probably yours,' his dander was up.

'Yes I know she is less than half my age. Don't you wish you were in my shoes?'

'My children? Which? The ones I already have or the ones we shall have?'

'That's my business and you are incredibly impertinent,' he was by now shouting.

'No, I shall not appeal! We shall get married, whatever you decide.'

'How? That is no longer your business.'

When I came back into the office, he said, more calmly, 'I shall frame the application and it will remind us of what fools they are in HQ.'

If I had had any doubts about marrying Bert, these had been allayed – and all the office now knew about our engagement. I wrote to mother and told her that I was engaged to marry an English Officer. Her reply was immediate – congratulations, could she have a photo – and I just had to get married at home.

I told Bert what mother had written. 'What a lovely idea,' he said. 'We'll do just that. The Army cannot stop me getting married in Czechoslovakia.'

But the logistics were quite horrendous. That did not discourage either Bert or me. First of all, I had to get back to

Czechoslovakia. Then Bert had to get there. On paper that looked very simple but it wasn't. I had no papers, except a DP Pass, an Identity Document issued to Displaced Persons. It was a long journey, involving going from the British Zone through the American Zone and then into another Country.

We had decided to consult the Czechoslovak *Chargé d'Affaires* at Bad Oyenhausen. Several months before we had made an abortive journey there, when due to a blown out tyre our car skidded, missed a bus, turned over several times and we had to be transported back in an Army lorry, the car being a complete write-off. Bert emerged unscathed while I injured the top of my spine, the results of which have stayed with me. We hoped this time we would be luckier. It was now the beginning of July 1946.

The *Chargé d'Affaires* had a proposition for me. At the racecourse at Dortmund were a large number of Czechs, all male, waiting to be repatriated. Somebody – an official person - had to go with them. Would I be willing to take charge of the transport? I marvelled at his confidence in me, aged just twenty-two.

It was anticipated that they would leave in about two weeks' time when formalities had been completed and a train procured. I could be housed in the hospital, next to the racecourse. I would be given every facility; the train would go to Prague, where I would hand over the refugees and my responsibility would end. I would be issued with a voucher for onward travel to Bratislava. Naturally, they would also provide me with an official pass.

How innocent we were; neither Bert nor I anticipated any problems. We drove back to Paderborn, I packed, said my goodbyes and, at the weekend, Bert's driver took me to Dortmund, to the hospital. There, I was given an airy room, overlooking the racecourse buildings where the refugees were housed. We had a picnic meal in my room, before we said goodbye and arranged to stay in telephone contact, until I actually left.

I went down to the racecourse buildings. They had been divided into large dormitories, most of which were deserted at this time of the day. I spoke to some of the group leaders, big swarthy men, who said that they had the men well under control and that they would see to it that there were no problems on the journey. They were all looking forward to going home. I realised that I was in charge of a transport of gypsies, or Roma as we now call them. I went back to my room.

A couple of days later, late in the evening when it was dark, a commotion broke out in the camp. Through the open window I could hear raised voices but they settled down after a while. In the morning I went to enquire what had happened. I was assured that everything was in order, but that the men were getting a bit restless, wanting to go home. I told them that we were waiting for a train to be made available and that I had heard it was just a matter of days. It was not very exciting just hanging around and I could understand their impatience.

Every day I spoke to Bert and reassured him that – maybe tomorrow - I would be off and that I would phone him as soon as I knew we were going. But that was not what happened. Three nights later a great hubbub broke out in the camp; all the lights came on, there was shouting and screaming; a messenger came running; would I please come immediately. I was led to the back of the building, where a man lay in a pool of blood, clearly dead. I asked two men to stay there, went back to the entrance and phoned for the police – in spite of their entreaties not to do so. Dead bodies were not something I had bargained for.

The German police came. It was not a pretty situation. I interpreted for the men. What had happened was that in spite of prohibition, they had installed an illicit still and made spirits from potatoes. Several got drunk, a fight ensued, knives were drawn and for reasons nobody knew or was willing to tell, several people were injured and one of them died. The incident could have stopped the whole transport leaving while the machinery of the law worked out who was guilty and what the appropriate punishment should be.

I tried to phone the Czechoslovak *Chargé d'Affairs*, but could not reach him. Obviously, he was not in his office at night. I phoned Bert and asked him to find the official and get him to come here immediately. It was morning by the time he came – as did Bert. I told them that I was not willing to be in charge of 300 violent men on a journey lasting three days; nor was I prepared to delay my return home while waiting for the German court proceedings to run their course.

Bert added that he was not of a mind to expose me to such a mob; that if he had known what was expected of me he would never have agreed to it. As far as he was concerned I was to pack, go back to Paderborn and we would make alternative arrangements for me to go back home – with or without the help of the *Chargé d'Affaires*.

Later I heard that the *Chargé* had to take the transport to Prague on his own, because nobody else was willing to do so. I also heard later that Hugo had been waiting at the station in Prague to meet me and send me on to mother in Bratislava. The *Chargé* explained to him that I had gone back to Paderborn, but would not say why, which worried Hugo and Mother no end.

When we got back to Paderborn, Bert and I went to see the Colonel. I explained that I wanted to go home to my mother, not that I was going there to marry Bert. He said he would see what could be done. A couple of days later I was issued with a *laissez passer*, which was a type of international passport and a letter from the British Authorities asking the

167

American authorities to assist me on my way home. Bert acquired some American script and unofficial permission to take me by car to Nuremberg where the Nazi War Criminal Trials had just started and to which his friend, the police officer, had managed to obtain a ticket – it was the hottest show in town!

It was arranged that we would travel to Nuremberg overnight, ostensibly to the trials. The ticket allowed the officer and his German driver passage across the border between the British and the American sector. To have an interpreter with them was not deemed unusual, nor was it noticed that there were two British Officers. But beyond Nuremberg they could not go. Before we left, Bert gave me a supply of chocolates and several boxes of cigarettes. They were better than any currency. I also had food and fruit for the journey, which was likely to last at least twenty-four hours. We also had a serious talk.

Bert said, 'Look, we have lived here in a place and under conditions which were strange to both of us. It has been 'time out of context.' You may feel quite differently about me once you are home, among your own people, with your own family, in your own country. There may even be somebody there waiting for you. We have had a lovely time together. I love you but you must not feel under any obligation to me. I only want us to get married if you are quite certain that that is what you want, too.'

I told him, 'Let us give each other three months apart. Then, if you still want to marry me, you have to come to Bratislava and marry me there.'

THEY DROPPED ME OFF at Nuremberg railway station. There were no fond farewells, too many troops about. I asked Bert to send Mother a telegram that I was on my way. I found an American soldier, showed him my *laissez passer* and asked him about the next train to Prague. He told me that I had to go to American Army Headquarters and see somebody there. He could only let people through who had a proper ticket and it was not possible to buy a ticket for a train to Prague. He unbent sufficiently to tell me that there was a train in the sidings that was to go to Prague that night.

My main piece of luggage was a large wooden trunk with a domed lid and I also had a small suitcase. I found a porter with a handcart who was willing to take me and my luggage to the American Army Headquarters. On arrival, I asked the soldier at the door 'Who did I have to see to get a permit to travel to Prague?'

Fortune smiled on me when he said, 'It's Captain Benes you want.' A Czech name – perhaps even a Czech officer? I asked the porter to wait, told him I would pay him double, requested the soldier to keep an eye on him and not let him move or take my luggage anywhere and went in search of Captain Benes. Indeed, although he was American, he spoke Czech.

I explained my situation, showed my *laissez passer* and the letter from the Czech *Chargé d'Affaires*.

'Any other identification?' he asked.

I showed my identity pass from the DP camp.

'How come you are still here? Most people have gone home long ago,' he enquired.

'I have been working with the Military Government and Control Commission.'

'Was that better than going home?'

'I did not know what was waiting for me there,' I told him.

'What is waiting for you there is work to build a new country. Good luck!'

I was given a document to allow me to travel on the train and also a chit for food and drink in the canteen downstairs.

The Woman Without A Number

I went there, collected some sandwiches and a couple of doughnuts, drank some coffee and took the rest out with me. The porter was waiting and we started to walk back to the station. Partway I stopped and shared my sandwiches and doughnuts with him. At the station I showed my travel document and was told where the train was. The porter and I found it. It was not empty but was bringing students back who had been stranded in France since the beginning of the war. Or that was what they said. There were people in all compartments.

I went along all the carriages; the best I could find was one with only two young people, a boy and a girl. They were not too pleased to see me, because they had hoped to stretch themselves out on the seats throughout the journey and sleep. I paid the porter and gave him a bar of chocolate and he was profuse in his thanks. The trunk was a problem, it could not be left in the corridor so the lad helped me to push and pull it into the carriage, where it acted as a sort of table over which we had to climb. At least it would stop anyone else coming in.

The boy and the girl had not been exactly friendly when I had arrived and interrupted their *tête-à-tête* but a couple of bars of chocolate and the offer of an English smoke thawed the atmosphere to a certain extent. It got dark. We were still in the sidings. The couple settled head to toe and covered themselves in their blanket. I lay down on my side and covered myself with my coat. We drifted off to sleep.

We were woken by shouts and movements of the carriages. We were shunted onto a main line, coupled to a long train and we were off.

THERE WAS A TEARFUL welcome, obviously, when I arrived in Bratislava. I did not recognise my brother Tomy and my cousin Magda who had come to meet me. They had

170

both been just twelve years old when I left. They were now sixteen and seventeen had been through a lot and looked like adults. Mother could not come to the station – somebody had to mind the shop, someone had to earn a living.

We went home, back to 51 Palisady; up those many steps, dragging my trunk. When Tomy opened the door, it seemed – almost – as if nothing had changed. But it had, lots of things were missing.

The large white Carrara marble fireplace in the sitting room had been replaced with a rough red brick one. The apartment had been requisitioned by the Germans and then by the Russians. When I looked up I saw that the large twelve-branch crystal chandelier was also gone.

When still at home, I had embroidered, in petit point, the seats and arms of three of the rosewood Rococo chairs. The small settee still had its faded regency satin and was waiting for me to recover it. The furniture in mother's bedroom was different. It was the pear-wood suite which had belonged to Magda's parents, Uncle George and Aunt Janka. It was too big – and too yellow – for anyone to take a fancy to it. There was now a sofa in the dining room where Tomy slept. Magda slept on the sofa in front of Mother's big bed. It had been the bed of her parents, who had not returned from Auschwitz. I often wondered how she felt about it but one didn't ask questions or talk about the recent past.

My own room no longer had the beautiful Biedermayer dresser with its secret drawers; and the dressing room next door, where the Fraulein used to sleep, stood empty. The parquet floors were bare, all the Persian carpets had gone, as had the Khelim rugs which had framed the windows. But it was not a bad beginning. We were oddly ill at ease after greeting and embracing each other. Too much had happened, too much lost. Magda was keen to know about Bert, my fiancé, when were we getting married, could she be my bridesmaid. I told her that I did not yet know about the wedding but, when it happened, she most certainly would be my bridesmaid. Tomy wanted to know whether I would help mother in the shop so that he could carry on with his studies, he wanted to be an engineer, like his grandfather and Magda, to my surprise, an architect.

'Not a solicitor, like your father?' I asked.

'Certainly not. Laws change all the time, you never stop learning or you are out of business. If you lose a case, the client won't pay. No, I want to build things,' she said.

The sad thing was she never did become an architect. Life had different plans for her.

When mother came home there were more tears. I was also reproached: 'Why did you not come before?' she asked. 'You could have been here with us a year ago!'

'Yes,' replied Magda, 'but then she would not have had an English Officer as her fiancé.'

Mother had brought packages and packages of food, she had never been an enthusiastic cook nor had Magda. I could and anticipated, wryly and correctly, that I would be the one to keep them fed – and to keep the place clean. During the next week I searched for my friends. None of the men had returned; Iby and Lizzy, Uncle Imre's daughters had, and of my school friends, only Susie Sonnenfeld. That was it. Any of the others who had survived had emigrated to Australia or what was to become Israel. I had no empathy with the native Slovaks but there were a few youngsters and teenagers about, potential partners for Tomy and Magda.

Bratislava, after the war, was a bleak place. There was rationing, a black market, a lot of un-cleared rubble, bomb damage, everything looked tired and unkempt. I had never been very fond of the place and was even less so now. I could not see how I could continue to live there. Then the letters started to arrive. Bert wrote every day, sometimes twice a day. The flimsy pale blue airmail letters usually arrived in batches. I would sort them into date order before reading them. His beautiful handwriting was reduced in size to bare legibility so as to fit as much as possible onto each page.

He wrote about what he did, what he saw, what he thought, naturally also about the weather, about the funny things that happened and interwoven in the text, every instance when something reminded him of me or he thought of me or wondered what I would have thought or done. I had never had love letters before and had no way of judging them but I am certain that they were the most beautiful ones imaginable.

In Germany, in the Army, it was not done to show affection in public. Bert and I had never held hands, embraced, kissed or even touched in public. We had developed a private code to affirm our feelings to each other.

One of us would ask, 'May I ask the time-honoured question?'

To which the answer was either, 'Yes,' or 'Yes, but not now' or if we felt like teasing each other, 'I can't see why.'

In his mischievous way, Bert would even mention it while questioning a suspect in Court, which made it quite difficult to answer without blushing.

What was the time-honoured question? 'Do you love me still?'

Every letter had at least one or two instances of this question. The word love, as such, was not mentioned. It was one of the few words Bert found difficult to voice, the other one was sorry.

If I had not been in love with Bert before, then I fell in love with him through his letters. I kept them for years and years, in a shoebox. In one of our many moves the box disappeared – I think it was in the move from Downend to

Reading, when Bert supervised it at the Downend end and a lot of things did not reappear in Reading.

But he consoled me, 'You don't need those old letters; you've got me now.'

'It's not the same thing,' I wailed.

There had never been any doubts in Bert's mind that he wanted to marry me. By the time November came I knew that my future lay with him and I wrote to him, asking whether a date at the beginning of December would suit him for our wedding. Could he organise matters his end, I would see to everything at mine. A telegram came in reply: 'I'll be with you as soon as I can arrange it.'

TO ARRANGE A WEDDING at a month's notice is bordering on lunacy. As the Army had refused him permission, that was an avenue we did not intend to explore again. By this time, Army Officers could travel to Prague for rest and relaxation. Bert had met up with a Capt. Popper who came originally from Prague and who was keen to revisit the city and renew contacts there. They decided to travel together and applied for permission to visit which was granted. Since there was no direct rail connection between Paderborn and Prague, they had to go by car to Nuremberg to catch a train. I had successfully completed this journey a couple of months earlier, so they did not anticipate any problems.

I needed Bert's birth and medical certificate, as at this time you had to have a clean bill of health to marry, as well as Win's death certificate so that I could apply for a Special Licence, because Bert would not be here long enough for the normal process. A special licence could be obtained three days before the wedding but the papers had to be submitted two weeks in advance of the proposed date of marriage. Since that date depended on when Bert actually arrived, it was imperative to submit the papers as soon as possible. I managed to get my birth certificate and had my medical details and, by mid-November, the requisite documents had been submitted to the Mayor's office.

I visited the British Consulate which was around the corner from where we lived and explained the situation to them. The Consul told me that under the present British laws a marriage conducted by the Czechoslovak authorities would not be recognised as legal in Britain. I had to let him know the actual date of the civil wedding and he would be present and would also supply an official interpreter for Bert and himself. After that Bert and I were to come to the consulate where he would conduct a wedding ceremony according to British Civil Law for which he would also supply the witnesses and he would then issue a British Certificate of Marriage. So, that was two weddings planned.

Next, Bert sent a telegram to say that the Army would only recognise a Church wedding. I hared back to the British Consulate. They could not resolve the problem but thought that the British Embassy in Prague would be able to. After a lot of telephoning and correspondence it was agreed that a Church of Scotland clergyman, who was attached to the Embassy, would be willing to come to Bratislava to conduct a Church of England wedding ceremony, provided I could find a church which would allow it to take place there.

Since neither I, nor any member of my family, had ever set foot in a Protestant church, this needed some sorting. I remembered that, when I went to primary school, there was a Protestant church not far away. I set out to find it then searched out the priest and explained the situation to him. He could not see a problem, particularly as I promised him a decent donation. The church was provisionally booked and I wired Bert accordingly. He replied that he would bring the necessary Army forms for this wedding with him. So now we had three weddings; the knot would be truly, firmly tied.

Mother made a list of all the things which had to be bought for my *trousseau*.

'You don't think I'm letting you go to England fitted out any other way than suitably and appropriate to our status?' she said. 'I won't have his family looking down on us.'

'But mother, Bert has been married before,' I told her. 'There is a house fully furnished and fitted out.'

'It doesn't matter,' she continued. 'It could not possibly be to your taste. I'll send a railway container with furniture, carpets, tableware, linen and bedding, besides your personal things.'

'But mother, there really is no hurry. I am not going to England yet.'

'Just as well, I can't do miracles.'

But mother did, nearly.

I had a wedding outfit made but I refused to be married in white brocade. After all, it was winter and I was not going to be betrothed with a nose blue from the cold. Instead I had a wool costume in greyish green with a white blouse and a white turban, which was most fashionable, draped with a short veil. I made the blouse myself from a white silk parachute I had brought back with me from Germany.

On my wedding day, Bert gave me a Victorian brooch with pearls and amethysts which had been his mother's. I pinned it to the blouse. My going-away outfit was a dark blue Chanel costume, with a dark blue coat lined in fur and a mink collar, muff and hat, together with beautiful pure silk underwear all hand stitched with handmade lace and similar nightwear and negligees.

We fixed the date for the 3rd December; Bert was due to arrive on the 30th November which would allow the statutory requirement of his local residence of three days.

The Mayor, not the Registrar, conducted weddings in Bratislava at the time and he was booked for 10am; the consul and interpreter were informed, the church was reserved for 1.30pm, the clergyman notified and the wedding breakfast at the Carlton Hotel was arranged for 3pm. The reception at home was to be between the ceremonies, at 11.30. Everything was planned with military precision, but things did not quite go to plan.

Also I forgot about wedding photographs.

I had stipulated that the news of my wedding should not be publicised. There were no announcements in the papers and word-of-mouth only to those friends who were invited to the wedding or reception. They were told that it was a private affair. The wedding breakfast would be small and only the family, the witnesses, the clergyman and the British Consul with his interpreter invited, not more than a dozen people.

After I had come home, I had been besieged by reporters who had heard from my half cousin Iby and from others about my experiences, especially what they termed 'my heroism' in the camp. I refused to co-operate, I wanted none of it; it was not something I felt I needed to be proud about and I certainly did not want it all brought up again and capped with my wedding to an English Officer. But a girl I had been at school with and who was now a reporter on the local paper, did hear about it. She said it was too good a story not to be told.

I had not mentioned to anyone that, as far as the British Army was concerned, we were forbidden to marry and that any advance publicity could very well have scuppered our plans. Instead, I explained that it would embarrass Bert and would spoil our day. I told her that I would invite her to the wedding and to the wedding breakfast so that she could have the complete story provided she promised not to write anything about it until after Bert had left. She agreed and kept her word, so there were thirteen people at my wedding breakfast.

Everything was now in place, only Bert had to arrive and this was when miracles were needed. He and Carl Popper managed to get railway tickets from Nuremberg to Cheb on the Czechoslovak border. Each was allowed to take only £10 in currency with him. They filled up their car with petrol and, although it was not permitted, also the boot with jerry cans because they would have to drive through the American Zone and had no means of getting fuel from the American authorities, things were very territorially organised.

They were driven by Bert's German driver, whom he trusted implicitly. They also brought food for the journey, including some tins of corned beef, coffee and cigarettes which could be used, if need be, to barter with. The plan was that they would be driven to Nuremberg, the driver would return to Paderborn and they would ring him up from Nuremberg on their return, hoping he would be able to collect them. It was all left rather in the air.

On arrival at Nuremberg they reported, as I had, to the American authorities for permits to travel on the train. The Americans had been helpful to me but were less so to them. First, they doubted the validity of their travel vouchers; indeed they doubted that they were British Officers because they could not envisage why they would want to travel to Prague for R & R when all of Germany, France, Belgium and Holland were there for their pleasure. Bert could not really tell them that he was going there to get married and Popper that he wanted to check whether any of his property had survived the war.

Eventually, grudgingly, they agreed to let them travel but, in spite of having vouchers for first class tickets, as befitted officers, they were put into a crowded third-class carriage with private soldiers. It was an unusual experience for both of them and it was not until the journey was part-way over and the soldiers had left the train that they found seats in a first class carriage but were asked to pay extra for this privilege. So went their £10 allowance.

It was late evening when the train arrived at the border between the American Zone of Germany and Czechoslovakia. Their tickets were only valid for travel up to this point, to Cheb. Bert had sent me a telegram indicating on which train they were likely to be, but train travel was still uncertain and there was only one a day from Germany to Cheb. I travelled up there the day before the train was due, just in case. I had some business to transact at a bicycle factory there where only a personal intervention and a tin of English cigarettes ensured that we were going to get a consignment of bicycles for the shop within a week rather than, perhaps, in a month's time.

I was at Cheb station in the evening, went to the station master's office and asked him whether it was possible to check if there were two British officers on the train from Germany, which was due in shortly and was probably now at the border. It was no problem. He phoned the border post where the passports of all passengers were being inspected, listed and stamped. Bert and Popper were not on the train.

I went back into Cheb, phoned mother and spent the next twenty-four hours exploring a cheerless place, half the houses empty, because the Sudeten Germans had been deported to Germany. Many of their houses were now occupied by gypsy families.

The next evening found me again at the station. This time the answer to the station master's query was yes: there were two British Officers on the train and if I knew them, could I please get to the border because they could not make themselves understood and had no tickets to get them beyond Cheb. I got a taxi from the station to the border but the border guards did not want to allow me on the train because it had not yet been cleared by customs. I explained that I had come to meet the British Officers and that put a different complexion on it. I boarded and was greeted by two relieved faces. They did not know what they would have done if I had not turned up. I explained to the guards that I would pay their fares to Prague.

Eventually the train set off.

I asked the guard why the train had been held so long at the border. He explained that customs had to be thorough. There was also an hour's time difference between Germany and Czechoslovakia and due to the comprehensive search, the train was running late and I realised, with dismay, that this meant we would miss our connection to Bratislava. We would not get there in time for Bert to register and, if he didn't do so, there would be no wedding on the third.

I had a brainwave. On the next day a war criminal trial was due to start in Bratislava. What if Bert was going there to report on it? He could not possibly miss the start of it. I told Bert that he and Carl Popper were now the official reporters for *The Times*. They asked whether that could not be the *Telegraph*, but I told him that everybody would know of *The Times*. I found the guard and spoke to him. Half an hour later he came to our carriage and told us that the train to Bratislava would be held up until we arrived, that we would be taken to the train without delay on arrival in Prague. When the train arrived there, three porters ran along, grabbed our luggage and took us across the railway lines to the sleeper to Bratislava which stood there with steam up. Popper had to fight to keep his own luggage from being spirited onto the Bratislava train. Bert, our luggage and I were manhandled into it and it set off.

It was 10.30pm; the train was now thirty minutes late. Bert and I looked at each other and burst out laughing. I had tickets for a double cabin. The guard showed us to it, where the beds had been made up. We were both rather hungry by now. I had brought salami, smoked goose and cheese from home and bread in Cheb and a couple of bottles of beer. In the corridor were folding seats with tables. We sat down and did justice to the food.

There was some discussion on who should have the top berth but it did not develop into an argument. Bert, always the gentleman, said, 'I'll go on top.'

'Really?' I replied, dryly.

Mother was waiting for us at the station when the train got in at six in the morning and it was home to breakfast. Mother and Bert hit it off from the word go; I had been apprehensive about that. My little Maltese terrier puppy Cherie also took to Bert, taking a particular liking to his feet and trying to lie on his stockinged feet, if at all possible.

After breakfast I took Bert to register with the Police and then, with the relevant document, the train ticket confirming entry into Czechoslovakia on the previous day and his personal identity papers, to the Mayor's office to get the Special Licence.

We nearly did not get it. The official wanted to take the date of registration as Bert's first day in Czechoslovakia which would have meant a wedding on the fourth, whereas all the arrangements had been made for the day before. It took a lot of talking, the discrete transfer of an envelope and a tin of Players' cigarettes to get the Special Licence needed.

I then took Bert to the Hotel Carlton, now the Radisson, where Mother had booked a suite. When I took my grandchildren in 2006 for their first visit to Bratislava that is where we also stayed. Nothing but the best – one had to make certain that the English husband saw that his bride came from the top – or nearly the top – drawer. Mother had arranged for Bert to stay at the Carlton before the wedding, and that the wedding breakfast would also be held there. I would join Bert after the wedding and we would have two nights in Bratislava. Then we would go to Prague, to stay in the Hotel Adlon. We would do some sightseeing, Hugo would take Bert to a football match - Sparta Prague were playing - and then I would see Bert back off to Germany. Since there had not been time to arrange a stag or hen party, the younger members of the family and friends had arranged a night out for both of us in a night club on the evening before the wedding.

It was a tight programme but Mother was very efficient, so it was bound to work out.

I WAS FEELING SLIGHTLY fragile after the party the night before and wondered how Bert was. He had discovered that there were lots of other drinks beside whisky available in Bratislava and he had tasted most of them. I did not hear from him initially but then I did not expect to. The plan was that at 9.30am Uncle Imre was to go to the Hotel Carlton to collect Bert. The only drawback was that Uncle Imre spoke German, Hungarian and Slovak; Bert only English and they had not met before. Fortunately Bert was the only person in a British Army Officer's uniform waiting in the foyer, so he must be the groom. Uncle Imre enquired at the desk whether the clergyman had arrived. Nobody knew and Uncle Imre had no way of asking Bert whether he had met him.

As it is only a few minutes' walk to the Town Hall, they arrived there in time. I was not far behind them. It was a cold morning in early December so I decided to wear my going-away outfit and a fur-lined coat rather than the wedding one. I was relieved to see Bert and Uncle Imre as well as the British Consul and the official interpreter. At this stage there was no need for the clergyman to appear, so I was not worried. There seemed to be a lot of other people about, most of whom I don't know but mother does and she waved to them.

The Registry Office wedding – slightly longer than usual because everything has to be translated into and from English for Bert and the Consul – proceeded otherwise without a hitch. The interpreter's English was quite atrocious. I looked at Bert and he winked at me; I would have done this much better. We were soon married in accordance with Czechoslovak law and graciously accepted congratulations.

Mother and the family went home to await the guests who had been invited to the reception. Bert and I took a taxi to the British Consulate for wedding number two.

We now went through a British civil wedding ceremony; the consul being empowered to marry people. Two employees of the Consulate acted as witnesses and the Consul congratulated us. He proceeded to fill out a British passport and handed it to me. From the moment I married Bert I became a British Citizen.

He advised me that, according to Czechoslovak law, I had now relinquished my Czechoslovak citizenship by marrying a foreigner. I could apply to ask to retain it and have dual citizenship but he advised against it.

'We live in uncertain times,' he said. 'It could cause problems.'

I recalled the problems my father had while I was a child when he was still a Hungarian citizen but living in Czechoslovakia, and how he was frequently expelled when there were border disputes between the two countries. I couldn't imagine that happening between Britain and Czechoslovakia, but then, I wanted a new life, so there was

no reason whatsoever for me to retain Czechoslovak
citizenship. Two weddings down – only one more to go.

We walked the few steps home. The place was full of
well-wishers, drink flowing freely, canapés being consumed,
presents handed over and embraces exchanged. I only knew
half the people, maybe even fewer. People came and went,
as is usual at this sort of event. What Bert needed was a hair
of the dog, a stiff drink, and my cousin Iby's American fiancé
duly produced some Scotch whisky in a very large measure.
It was the first of many.

The front door was left open to admit anyone who
wanted to come and could brave the fifty-odd steps up to
our apartment. The door bell rang and the maid brought in
a man dressed in black, bearing a small suitcase. He spoke
English, the clergyman had arrived.

I asked him, 'Why did you not go by taxi to the hotel as
arranged?'

'I thought it better if I came direct from the station,
because we really should go through the service first,' he
responded.

The train must have arrived hours ago. I know, because
we booked the ticket and paid for it.

'Where have you been until now?' I enquired.

'I thought that the station would be in the town and I was
told that Palisady was just outside the city centre. I thought
I'd see something of the town.'

'But the station is miles outside the town!' I said
incredulously. 'Didn't anyone tell you? It must have taken
you ages to walk and you wouldn't have seen anything of
the town.'

He nodded and replied wryly, 'You are right.'

'You must be hungry and thirsty,' I said.

He agreed and readily accepted the sandwiches and
coffee but not Bert's whisky. Bert advised him that he had

been married before so did not really need to go through the practice before the ceremony. Perhaps he thought that valuable drinking time was being wasted and he did seem rather anxious to get back to the drink and the party.

The clergyman would have none of it. 'When was that?' he asked. When Bert told him it was in 1923, he snorted, 'You'll have forgotten most of it – and there are also changes. It will do you good to go through it.'

I had read through the Anglican wedding service carefully in Germany when I thought we would be married there but the clergyman had taken a lot of trouble to come to us, travelling overnight from Prague and returning on the night train. I decided that it would be churlish not to do as he wanted. So, we went through the service – who stands where – who says what.

It was agreed that Bert and the clergyman would go back to the hotel in a taxi to have a rest and refresh themselves and that they would be collected at 1pm by Uncle Imre and taken to the church. The clergyman said he preferred to walk but asked Bert to take the case which contained his vestments and copies of the Order of Service. I went to speak to the guests still here, had some coffee and a sandwich and then went to change.

The second problem was with the flowers. I had wanted white roses. Mother had white roses at her wedding so I wanted the same but, in early December 1946, they were not easy to obtain. They had to be flown in from Holland and when they arrived, the tips of the buds were blackened by frost. Early in the morning the florist rang me and told me about it.

'I can't use them,' he said. 'They are awful.'

'What other white flowers do you have?' I asked, disappointedly.

'Do they have to be white?'

'Yes, of course' I said.

'Well, I have white chrysanthemums.'

'No, no,' I cried, 'those are funeral flowers.'

'I do have some white lilacs but that is not a usual flower in a bridal bouquet. Are you certain you would not like red carnations? I have plenty of those.'

A bouquet of white lilacs arrived as I was changing; Magda the bridesmaid, got the red carnations. It was now nearly one o'clock. Uncle Imre went to fetch Bert and the clergyman to bring them to the church. Mother, Tomy – who was slightly miffed because he wanted to give me away but was vetoed by me and mother as being too young at sixteen to be the father of the bride – and Magda, my bridesmaid, left for the church.

At the appointed time, twenty-to-two, Hugo and I arrived at the church. The door was open but there was no welcoming clergyman, no sign of life. Hugo went in to check on the situation. He came back slightly puzzled and told me that the congregation was all there but no Bert, no Uncle Imre and no clergyman. That was odd. The clergyman should have been waiting at the door for me. He seemed a slightly peculiar person. Maybe he had also walked to church and was therefore late, but Bert and Uncle Imre should surely be there by now. I told the driver to go round the block and return ten minutes later, but nothing had changed. Where were they? Had they gone to the wrong church? Once more around the block; still nothing.

I told Hugo, 'This is impossible! They must be here.'

Hugo and I marched down the aisle and into the vestry to find the clergyman, suitably robed. He and the groom were discussing England's chances in the Test Match then being played in Australia. Bemused, Uncle Imre, not understanding a word, was standing by and probably thinking that this was an integral part of English wedding ceremonies. My arrival rather disrupted the conversation.

'Do you think you could continue this conversation later?' I asked, somewhat sarcastically. 'Do you think we might do the wedding now?'

'Good God, just look at the time! Profuse apologies!' the clergyman pleaded.

Contrary to custom, the clergyman led the bride, groom, the best man and Hugo, taking the place of the father of the bride, in procession from the vestry to stand in front of the Altar. Since none of the congregation had ever been at a Church of England wedding before, nobody knew that it was not a weird English custom. I knew better, but this is the third wedding of the day, so the main thing was to get it over with.

The Church of Scotland parson conducted the marriage according to the rites of the Church of England in a Protestant church, so that the British Army's requirements for a valid wedding should be met.

The clergyman was naturally invited to the wedding breakfast and the discussion about the Test Match continued between him and Bert during the meal. Indeed, in his speech, the clergyman referred to it in great detail. Having heard about our abortive efforts to get married in Germany, he mentioned that in spite of a sticky wicket we played with a straight bat and did not let ourselves be caught in the slips. The whole of this was puzzling even to those of us who understood English but were unfamiliar with the religion of cricket, including me, and totally incomprehensible to all the others.

Next came the wedding breakfast. A different wine was served with each of the eight courses. The waiter discovered during the first course that Bert rather liked Czech beer so, along with the appropriate wine, he got a tall glass of beer with every plate. That, together with the several measures of whisky he had during the reception and the wedding rehearsal meant that when Bert and I retired to our suite afterwards, he threw himself across the bed and fell asleep.

A little while later, a timid knock on the door revealed the clergyman asking for his suitcase so that he could return, job well done, to Prague. He had no chance to give his *adieus* to a snoring Bert. I had put a book into my case but had not thought I would read it on the first night of my married life. First I took off Bert's shoes and loosened his belt. He was dead to the world, which included me. I had a luxurious bath with lots and lots of scented liquids then changed into a flimsy silk nightdress and a seductive negligee, trimmed with marabou feathers. I took the book out of my case, opened the bottle of champagne that was waiting for us in its ice bucket, and drank it on my own, reclining on the settee in our suite.

Later on, I managed to move Bert to his half of the bed without him being aware of it and went to bed myself. I did not have to be careful; nothing could have woken him.

Next morning I rang room service and asked for breakfast to be sent up with some much needed Alka-Seltzer tablets. I then went to wake Bert. That was when I realised that we had forgotten all about the wedding photographs. I phoned Mother. In Czechoslovakia, it was not usual at that time to have photos taken outside the church or the Registry Office after a wedding. The new couple would, more likely, adjourn to a photographer's studio and have formal pictures taken there. Our wedding day had been so full that I had forgotten that a studio session had been booked for 6pm. Mother phoned me back an hour later while we were still having breakfast, to say that it was now booked for us at 11am. After eating, I again dressed in the suit I had worn for the wedding, put the hat and my bouquet into a hatbox and we went off to have our photos taken. Just another example of Mother's fiendish efficiency. As a thank you, Mother and

I sent the clergyman a dressed turkey for Christmas, knowing that the British like the tradition and that this bird was scarce in Prague. But Czech turkeys bear little resemblance to the fat English one; they are rather scrawny, so I wonder what they made of it at the embassy.

IN THE END, WE had just that one day in Bratislava before we took the night train to Prague and booked into the Hotel Adlon. In the morning I took Bert sightseeing as Hugo was not free. In the evening, Hugo joined us for dinner. Later on, Bert insisted that he join us in our room and a heavy drinking session ensued between the men.

The next day, Sunday, we went to the Hradcin, the Prague castle and to the cathedral in the castle, where we were fortunate to see the enthronement of the new Archbishop. Using the mirror in my compact and standing with my back to the altar, which was far away in the distance, I managed to see quite a bit over the heads of the crowded congregation, all standing, and most of them, like me, with their backs to the ceremony using the same means of viewing. That afternoon, Hugo took Bert to the football match of the season. In the meantime I packed and paid our bills because Bert was leaving on the night train to Nuremberg and I was going back to Bratislava.

Hugo and I took Bert to the station where he was reunited with Carl Popper. I had packed some food for them for the journey, made certain that the tickets were in order and that they were in the right compartment.

We said our goodbyes, neither of us certain when we were going to see each other again but whenever it was, it would be in England. Bert's posting to the Control Commission was supposed to end in March and I was to plan on getting to England about the same time. My train left about two hours after Bert's. Hugo and I sat and had a coffee while waiting. All of a sudden the enormity of what I had done hit me, I had taken an irrevocable action to split from the past.

Whereas most brides have their doubts before their wedding, I had mine afterwards. I don't know what Hugo made of my tears, I assured him that they were not caused by my split from my new husband but by grief about my forthcoming separation from what was and what might have been. He was certain, having now got to know Bert, that I had made the right decision.

I realised on the train to Bratislava that we had forgotten to notify the police of Bert's departure. I put this out of my mind; I did not think it likely that he would come back to Czechoslovakia so it would not matter. That he did and it did matter belongs to another story. After such a hectic week it seemed somewhat of a letdown to get back to normal.

Mother now really got into gear. She had seen some beautiful furniture and china in an exhibition in Prague and I was to take the bedroom suite in Canadian birds-eye maple to England, as well as the hand-painted Karsbad porcelain service in lapis lazuli and gold, and ten dozen cut glass crystal glasses, suitable for all occasions. She also wanted me to take the silver tableware and cutlery she had been given on her marriage because it went from daughter to daughter. One could not know whether it would be possible for me to collect it on her death, so it would be better if it went with me as part of my dowry.

Mother decided that nothing but hand-woven linen would do for sheets, unless they were damask. She had a dozen woven and bought another dozen in pink damask, each item had to have my initials embroidered on it. The same applied to table linen and nothing but the best damask would do for that either.

Big square pillows filled with goose down, large quilted bed covers, embroidered vanity sets – you name it – it was bought or made ready for my new life. I had no idea where mother got the money from and, when I asked, she told me that this was not something to concern me.

I was taken to be fitted for more and more outfits; spring, summer, autumn and winter ones. I was measured and fitted for hand-made shoes and boots in black, dark brown and tan. Leather handbags in the same colours and matching gloves and hats, twelve nighties and six negligées and twelve sets of knickers and petticoats – everything in pure silk trimmed with lace. It was no use protesting, Mother had decided and organised it all. All this was to be packed into a railway container and to follow me to England because officially I was an Officer's wife being repatriated to England after the war and could therefore take my belongings with me.

Bert continued to write daily. There were problems for him, though, because the scam of the shadow cars had been discovered. The cars were speedily disposed of down ravines, in woods and rivers, their identification marks removed. Everybody was interrogated but most of the culprits, Regular or Short Service Officers, had by now left Germany and been demobbed and in the end it was decided, since even the Brigadier's driver had been involved to let the matter drop, except that everybody got a severe talking to.

Bert was now back in Büren, as resident officer, alone and bored to tears in the huge building. I was concerned about his drinking. Finally he heard that he had been posted back to the UK and was due to arrive in England by the 16th March, 1947. Could I arrange to travel to England so that my arrival would coincide with his? He had to report to the War Office.

The Woman Without A Number

I went to the consulate and explained the situation. The consul thought it could be done, possibly. He would book my travel through to Bristol where Bert's family lived and would also provide me with some foreign currency for the journey and for England, because currency was not obtainable by a private individual at this time in Czechoslovakia. He was as good as his word. I got tickets for the train from Bratislava to Vienna; first class sleeper on the Orient Express to Paris, connecting with the Blue Train from the Riviera to Waterloo. From there I would have to take a taxi to Paddington for the Bristol train.

FORTUNATELY, THERE WAS NO weight restriction on luggage on trains. I had two large suitcases; one for shoes, boots, bags and underwear, the other for suits, dresses and suchlike which has to be packed carefully so as not to crease. There was, naturally, also a hat-box, because no lady travelled without one and I had a beautiful pigskin overnight case, a present from Uncle Imre. I had no jewel case, because I had few jewels.

Mother had also, with her usual efficiency, packed a small case with food. 'You can throw it away when you have finished with the food,' she told me.

'There is bound to be food on the train,' I protested.

'Perhaps, perhaps not. It's best to be prepared.'

My whole family saw me off the next morning.

In Vienna Uncle Imre's daughter Lizzy met my train and saw me safely onto the Orient Express. What opulence! I had a compartment to myself and the settee was made up into a bed in the evening. My big cases travelled in the guard's van.

The winter of 1946/7 had been a particularly hard one. The Danube had frozen over and, starting from its delta in the Black Sea, had been bombed to break the ice up. It was feared that when the thaw set in upriver, it would cause flooding. There was flooding, anyway, but it would have been much worse. As I woke in the early hours and looked out of the window I noticed water as far as I could see. The train stopped frequently.

When I asked the guard what was happening, he told me that it had to be diverted from its normal route because of the floods.

'Does this mean that we will be late in Paris?' I enquired.

'Oh, yes, there is no question about it,' he confirmed.

I was anxious because, according to my tickets, I was supposed to arrive there at the *Gare de l'Est* at 11am and to leave from the *Gare du Nord* at 2.30pm, a tight schedule.

'There is no chance of us getting to Paris before two at the earliest,' he said.

The train stopped again and again. The dining car had been detached some time before. The food, even for the first class passengers had not been tempting and I was glad of what mother had packed.

It was 6pm when the train finally drew into Paris, the train on which I had a reservation had left. I would have to spend the night in Paris and hope to get on the train the next day. I got a porter, my luggage and a taxi.

'Where to?' the driver asked.

I did not know the French capital and thought it best if I could get a room in an hotel near the *Gare du Nord*. I explained that to the cab driver and we set off.

The first hotel he tried and the next one were full. I finished up at the *Hotel de l'Opera*. Even today I have no idea where it is but it certainly was expensive. I explained to the Concierge that I was only staying overnight, so could my luggage be stored? It could and I was conducted to my room. It was small and most of it was taken up by an enormous bed. When I sat on the edge of it, my feet touched the wall but then three people could have easily slept in the bed. The bathroom was en suite and considerably bigger than the bedroom, all white marble, a huge bath, twin washbasins set in a white marble slab, a big mirror over and my first encounter with a bidet. I was hungry and felt dirty.

I had a quick bath, changed and descended the stairs in search of the restaurant.

When I opened the door marked 'Restaurant' I found myself in a bar entirely full of men.

A pageboy materialised, they seemed to be everywhere. He led me along corridors to the restaurant, marked *Salle à manger*. Should I have known? I wondered. It was about eight o'clock I hoped they had some food left especially as rationing was still a reality.

The dining room was large with only one table occupied. A majestic headwaiter approached with four others in train. He led me to the table furthest from the one already occupied. While he stood, one of the waiters pulled a chair out for me, the second re-positioned the table, the third opened the huge serviette and placed it on my lap and the fourth presented me with the menu. From his back pocket the headwaiter pulled a pad, from his breast pocket a pencil and stood poised to take my order. The menu simply informed me of what there was, not giving any choices. There was a soup, a dish I did not recognise, then potatoes, salad, coffee. I nodded and they all went off. A little while later, two waiters wheeled a serving trolly to my table and stood back waiting. The third waiter came carrying a soup terrine, followed by the fourth with a ladle on a salver. I was certainly getting the silver service treatment. The terrine was deposited on the serving table with the ladle. They in turn stood back as the headwaiter approached with dignity. A cup and saucer appeared, the cup was filled with a ladleful of liquid and placed before me. The headwaiter bowed, the others bowed, removed the terrine and the ladle and departed. One of the waiters approached again with a small basket covered with a white cloth and placed it before me. It contained a tiny bread roll.

The soup was a consommé which tasted as if it had been repeatedly diluted and it was not too warm either. Still, I was hungry and it did not take me long to finish the soup and the roll.

I waited. Two waiters appeared. One took the cup and saucer, the other placed my used side plate carefully in the basket and, in step, they marched away. I wondered if the hotel had been frequented by German officers who had encouraged the waiters to march in goosestep, rather than to slide, as was usual. The salad followed, two lettuce leaves and a little shredded cabbage. I was asked if I required a dressing and said I would. After a due interval, the procession reappeared this time with a covered dish. With ritual precision the contents were placed in a bowl on a large plate and placed in front of me. It looked extremely unfamiliar. There were no vegetables, nothing to go with it. Its texture was slightly rubbery, there was not much taste, molluscs of some sort in a rather nice sauce; certainly nothing I had eaten before, but I did now hoping all the time that I was not making a faux pas by starting before the vegetables arrived but I was too hungry to stand on niceties. Partway through, the procession reconfigured with a small dish containing two small plain boiled potatoes. Finally, something I recognised. A tiny cup of very weak coffee ended the meal. I gave the head-waiter the number of my room, told him to put it on my bill and got up from the table nearly as hungry as I had sat down.

Back in my room, I opened the case mother had so thoughtfully provided and from which I had already eaten a couple of things. This time I found a leg of roast duck, some sourdough bread and cut myself a piece of the hunk of cheese. That was followed by a piece of poppy seed cake and I was finally feeling human again. Mother had even thoughtfully provided a knife and some linen napkins. I was pleased to notice that there was still quite a bit in the case for the next day.

I slept very well that night and on waking, telephoned room service for breakfast. Coffee and two rolls arrived with a little pot of preserve which I again augmented from my provisions. I repacked and went down into Reception with my case. It was 8am and I had to get to London. I wasn't sure what train to catch or if I would have a reservation. I paid the bill which was astronomical but it did not worry me too much as the consul had told me that everything would be paid by the British Government, provided I kept all receipts.

A taxi was ordered, my luggage was recovered from the store, pageboys escorted me and into the first available taxi and off I went to the *Gare du Nord*. The hardest part was getting a receipt from the driver but, eventually, another hurdle was overcome. At the station a porter with a trolley materialised.

'The train to London,' I quizzed him.

'Not yet in,' he succinctly replied.

'Ticket office?' I asked.

I joined a queue. I had been briefed by Mother always to give part of the tip to porters at the start, it made them more amiable and they did not mind waiting then. I presented my ticket and started to explain but did not get far, I was overwhelmed by a flood of French, far beyond my comprehension. I lifted both hands and the tirade stopped.

'*Attendez*', I said and explained in simple language that I came from Vienna, that the Orient Express had been delayed on account of the floods.' I was interrupted, yes the floods

were messing up the whole train timetable. I continued. I
had not arrived until the evening and the train had gone.

'Indubitably; it leaves at 2.30pm,' I was told.

I had to get to London today I explained.

'Not possible,' came the reply. 'The Blue Train was
coming from Nice and every place had been booked for
weeks.'

'But my ticket is valid for the Blue Train at any time; it is
only my seat reservation I cannot use, *n'est-ce-pas*?' I
ventured.

Reluctantly, he agreed that this was indeed the case.

'But Madame, where will you sit? You cannot stand all
the way to Calais and then to London, it's too far.'

'I'll sit on my cases,' I told him.

'They have to go in the guard's van,' he responded.

'Then I shall travel in the guard's van as well.'

'Madame, that's impossible, that's not permitted.'

I was getting anxious and also somewhat impatient. I
was used to the insurmountable mountains bureaucracy
could throw up but this was getting beyond a joke. People
behind and around me were getting restless.

'Look,' I said, 'I can get on the train, yes?'

With a reluctant shrug of his shoulders he agreed.

'Then that is what I shall do. I'll travel in the corridor. I
might find a gentleman willing to give up his seat for part of
the journey.'

My ticket was duly stamped to validate it for the date. I
turned to the porter.

'I want some food. What can we do about the suitcases?'
I asked him. He assured me he would look after them as if
they were his own.

'Madame is very brave,' he said admiringly. 'I'll come for
Madame in the restaurant in good time.' Somehow I had not
appreciated the rarity of a female travelling alone.

I had coffee and more coffee and war-time croissants and the porter came as promised.

'We have to hurry, the train only stops for fifteen minutes,' he gasped.

First to the guard's van and he wanted to see my ticket.

'Seat number?' he queried.

'It does not matter' I said.

'I need it to put on these cases,' he continued.

'Then put zero,' I told him.

'There is no zero!'

'Exactly,' I glared, mixing frustration with exasperation.

Not comprehending, he gave me two chits for my big cases. The porter had already swung himself up into the first carriage with my hatbox and overnight case.

'Come, Madame, quickly,' he said.

He ploughed his way down the corridors, me in his wake. Through second class and then first class – no empty seat anywhere. At the end of the last carriage there was a door marked, 'Private – *Corps Diplomatique*'.

He dumped my two cases in front of it and swung himself off the train.

'Good luck, Madame, a safe journey.'

As the train moved off, I threw my last French banknotes to him. At least I was on and I knew it would not stop before Calais. Then the boat-train. Naively, I wondered whether they actually put this train on the boat, maybe lifting it with cranes? Did the passengers stay on board while this happened?

Eventually a ticket collector arrived. He was not too sure about me sitting on my case in the corridor but there was little he could do about it and I did not feel inclined to search for a gentleman who might give up his seat. The ticket collector knocked on the 'private' door and was admitted by what looked to me like the image of an English gentleman;

very tall, so thin he looked emaciated, pinstripe suit and waistcoat. He admitted the ticket collector, who left after a few minutes. A little while later, the thin Englishman re-emerged.

'May I introduce myself,' he began. 'I am Lord Harriman's aide.' He gave me his name and I promptly forgot it.

'The ticket collector told us that you had no seat reservation. How did that happen?'

I told him that I was travelling to join my husband, an Officer in the British Army, that yesterday's Orient Express was delayed due to floods and that I had therefore missed my connection on which I had a seat reservation.

'Where were you last night, then?' he asked.

'The *Hotel de l'Opera*,' I said

He nodded, it was obviously a suitable location. He asked me to wait but I could hardly do anything else. He returned.

'His Lordship would be delighted if you would join us.'

It turned out to be not a railway carriage but a sumptuous drawing room with comfortable easy chairs, small tables, wall lights and a bar. There were four or five men in the carriage and the aide performed the introductions. The only name I remembered was Lord Harriman. It was very warm in the carriage so I opened my coat.

'Would you like to take your coat off?' he said.

I was helped to take it off and a mink collar and musquash lining rang all the right bells. I knew that ladies in England – at least in the England the two Misses Letters spoke about – always kept their hats on, so I did the same. Otherwise, except for Officers' mess etiquette, I was completely at sea as to how to behave in such exalted company. I had read in the papers before I left home that Lord Harriman was on a diplomatic mission somewhere on the Continent. I wished I had paid more attention to the article, it could have provided a useful topic of conversation but he was more interested in me and my story.

I had to self-censor it. I was going to a new life and did not want to take old baggage with me. My tale got somewhat abbreviated and certainly no mention was made of concentration camps. I told him that I had met Bert while working as an interpreter with the Control Commission in Germany, that he came to Bratislava to marry me and that he had been posted back to England. I was travelling to join him.

'How romantic!' exclaimed the aide. 'Will he meet you at Waterloo?'

'I do hope so; at least that is what we have arranged.'

'Is this all the luggage you have?'

'No, I have two cases in the guard's van and the rest is being shipped by container,' I continued.

I seemed to be pressing all the right buttons.

His Lordship turned to the aide and bade him to attach CD (*Corps Diplomatique*) labels to my cases so that I should have no problem with customs when entering England.

'You are a very courageous young lady undertaking this journey on your own,' he said.

He did not stop to think that I really had no alternative. Nor did he realise that, although this journey may be daunting, it was chickenfeed compared to what I had been through already.

Somebody had been busy with a spirit lamp in a far corner of the carriage and, after an hour or so, tea appeared. Fine bone china cups, tiny sandwiches with some sort of paste between them and little biscuits accompanied it. I accepted a cup.

'Milk? Sugar?' I was asked.

I knew from experience that it was not likely to be fresh milk.

'Neither, thank you,' I demurred. 'Just plain tea.'

I was at a loss how to drink it, with little finger stuck out or tucked in? At home we tucked in, it was deemed ostentatious to do otherwise. But the Misses Letters always seemed to have their little finger out. I did as at home, as did everybody else. Time passed and it got dark outside. I asked how much further to Calais and was told about another hour or so. The sherry came out. Would I like a glass?

'Yes, please,' I said.

'Doloroso, amontillado or fino?'

'Fino, please.'

I was not aware that ladies usually have sweet sherry but I abhor any sweet drink. I took a sip.

'Tio Pepe?' I asked. My taste buds had not let me down. I got a nod of approval; another hurdle was overcome.

The train slowed down as we approached the quayside at Calais.

'Leave your cases here,' they told me. 'They'll be seen to and your others will also be all right. You have to go through passport control and then board the ship. Make sure you go into the first class lounge. We'll see you at Dover, our carriage will be the last one on the train. Join us there for the rest of the journey.'

I expressed my thanks and appreciation.

The ship was big, at least for me who had never been on a sea-going vessel before, nor even seen the sea, which filled the landscape and was grey and choppy. I went through passport control, then along the quayside and up a long gangplank. My ticket was inspected and I was directed to the first class lounge; the place was deserted. I waited until the ship set sail and then started to explore. Everybody was in the bar but it seemed not a place for me. In the dining room, the tables were set with white linen but, again, there was not a soul inside. I went up on deck to get some fresh air. It was dark, windy, wobbly and not at all pleasant. I found a door, went in and down some stairs into a different environment. It was crowded, smoky, noisy and smelt pervasively of something I had never come across before. I asked a steward what it was.

'It's fish and chips, madam,' he told me.

'Your ticket? I showed him it.

'Sorry Madam, you are in the wrong part of the ship. I'll take you back to first class.

The sea was getting rougher I was not certain how my stomach was going to cope, so I decided not to eat.

I arrived at Dover shaken and stirred, to put it mildly. It didn't feel like I was finally in England as I passed through another passport control. Feeling slightly unsteady, I walked along to the train and found the last carriage and familiar faces.

It did not take too long to reach Waterloo. Lord Harriman wanted to be reassured about my onward journey. I explained to him that Bert and I had made contingency plans. If he was not at Waterloo to meet me and had been unavoidably detained, which is always possible with the Army, I was to get a taxi to Paddington. There, on the platform for the Bristol train – whatever the time – his brother and sister-in-law would be waiting. I didn't know them, but they would know me. I had arranged to put Bert's regimental badge on the collar of my coat and a red silk scarf around my neck. I was commended for this detailed planning.

On arrival at Waterloo, I thanked Lord Harriman for his kindness.

'It's nothing,' he said. 'Anyone would have done the same. Good luck in England.'

The aide picked up my case and hatbox and hurried along to the guard's van. Two other members of staff were busy unloading suitcases, boxes and paraphernalia. Porters appeared, as if they had been drawn there by magnets. The aide commanded one with a trolley to pick up my two cases, now proudly sprouting CD labels, added to them my small case and hatbox, hurriedly wished me good luck and got caught up in sorting out their official baggage.

Now I was truly on my own as I walked with the porter to the end of the platform. No Bert. I waited. Still no Bert. Travellers were thinning out and the porter was getting impatient. Still no Bert.

'A taxi, please,' I decided.

The driver loaded my cases. I paid the porter, turned to the taxi driver, said 'Paddington, please' and got into the taxi.

The taxi driver spoke. To my horror I did not understand a single word he was saying. He repeated it and I replied, 'Sorry, I don't understand. Paddington, please.'

He shrugged his shoulders and I wondered what language the natives were speaking.

The taxi driver delivered me, after a bewildering drive, to Paddington station. I paid him, got a porter and asked him to take me to the platform from where trains went to Bristol; it must have been after nine o'clock. When we arrived at the ticket barrier I looked around for Bert. No Bert but a couple approached me.

'You must be Vi,' said the man. 'I am Frank, Bert's brother and this is Connie, my wife. Bert has been delayed and will not be here until tomorrow.'

Since the English had problems in pronouncing my first name Ibolyka and its abbreviation Iby always led to questions as to what it meant and how it was spelt, I had explained that Ibolyka is Hungarian for a small wild violet, which I became known as. To my horror, that had been abbreviated to Vi, which I loathed. Bert must have told his family that Violet was my name and all of them continued to call me Vi.

'Have you been waiting a long time?' I asked.

'We were here last night because we thought you might have arrived yesterday,' Frank said.

'Oh, I am so sorry, the train from Vienna to Paris was late because of floods, so I missed the connection by several hours and there was no other train until this one,' I apologised. 'When is the train for Bristol?'

'Not until ten o'clock, I'm afraid and it is also a slow train. We won't get into Bristol until about two in the morning.'

'Sorry,' I said again. 'Is there anywhere I can get some food? I did not feel like eating on the boat.'

'No, the station buffet has closed now but we brought some sandwiches and a flask of tea.'

Even meat paste sandwiches and sweet milky tea were welcome. It was quite a tricky situation. I had no idea how much or little Frank and Connie knew about me and I knew nothing whatsoever about them. We sat on a bench and I answered questions about my family, carefully avoiding anything which could have identified me as an ex-inmate of a concentration camp or an ex-Jew. Neither of those facts were to be disclosed to anybody in England, it was baggage neither I nor Bert needed. I did not wish to fan any possible prejudices; not being English was bad enough at this time. I wanted a clean slate to be filled by new experiences.

The train arrived, we entered the carriage and the train set off. As it was raining hard, there was little to see from the windows but the weather was a useful topic of conversation. I must have dozed off eventually, I was very tired.

On arrival in Bristol, after a lot of effort, Frank managed to get a taxi and we went to their home. Actually it was not their house but belonged to Connie's father who was, apparently, the meanest human being known in the West Country. Stories about his avarice were rife. As I got to know Bert's family better I was told by many of them.

204

It was a tall narrow house on the side of a steep hill. The bulb in the entrance hall was so dim that it barely broke the darkness and the place was icy. Connie asked whether I wanted a cup of tea. I declined, all I desired was a bed with a good fat eiderdown to warm me up.

Connie led me to a bedroom which had an equally dim bare light bulb hanging from the ceiling. Heavy dark velvet curtains were drawn across the window. The room was sparsely furnished, beside the bed there were two chairs and a huge wardrobe, a small rug either side of the bed with the rest of the floor covered in dark lino.

'I'll bring you a hot water bottle,' said Connie.

I wondered what that was. I opened the bed, there was no such thing as a feather eiderdown but hard blankets over coarse sheets and two hard pillows. Connie came with two grey stone vessels. These were the hot water bottles. She placed them inside the bed, one at the bottom and one halfway up.

'I had a warming pan in the bed yesterday, so it should not be damp,' she told me. 'The bathroom is along the passage. I'll show you.'

It was equally cold and uninviting.

'Is the water hot?' I asked. I wanted to get some of the dust of the journey off me.

'No, but I could boil you a kettle,' Connie replied. 'The geyser over the bath is too noisy to put on now.'

I told her not to bother, used cold water to rinse my face and clean my teeth and went back to my bedroom, hoping that the hot water bottles had done their job and had warmed the bed up. I undressed, looked at my thin silk nightie and negligee and wondered how I was going to get warm. In the end, being tired and young I slept.

NEXT DAY BERT ARRIVED, about midday. He told me to repack quickly and take just enough clothes for a few days because we were going back to London. He had to report to the War Office for his next posting and he was due two week's leave. At this time it was usual for officers to stay at the Regent Palace Hotel, which was then one of the top hotels in London and that was where we headed. I stayed at the hotel while Bert took himself off for his interview.

He came back rather pleased. He had been posted back to his own Regiment, the Duke of Cornwall's Light Infantry at its depot in Bodmin. Bert had a house in Truro, which was within daily commuting distance of the depot. The only problem was that it had been let to a naval officer's family while he was abroad and they would not vacate the place until June. That was a problem to be coped with in due course, first he was going to show me London.

When I was a little child, I loved to be told tales before going to sleep. Mother or Father always managed to stop at an interesting point. My response was always to ask, '*Und dann und dann und dann...?*' (and what happened then and then and then). To complete this story, however, it is necessary to know what went before. It will complete the circle and lead to an understanding of why I had to escape to Hungary in the first place.

PART FIVE

12

*

Family Background

My story starts with the place where I spent most of it, where I lived between the ages of three and 17, at No 51 Palisady in Bratislava, now the capital of the Slovak Republic. My recollections work in pictures, my memories are always visual; so I have to take you by the hand and ask you to come with me to Bratislava, also called Pressburg by the Germans and Pozsony by the Hungarians or, originally by the Romans, Posonium; as it was between 1926 and 1941.

From the town centre, going uphill, you come to a square at the top of which stands the presidential palace. The main road continues straight on to the railway station. There are several turnings off to the right, down towards Commercial Street, but if you turn left just after the Café Stephanie, you come into the part of the town where the embassies are. The road, lined with mature plane trees leads up to the ruins of the castle; the upper section of the road is called Palisady, presumably the palisades protecting the castle had been here. On the right hand side at the beginning of Palisady was the German Staats gymnasium, a high school where the teaching language was German, which I attended for three years. Opposite, just round the corner, is the British Embassy. Except for the Embassy precincts, two or three storey blocks of apartments line the street and there are also one or two villas. Palisady 51 is such a block. Beside the concierge's flat, there are eight apartments, six fronting the street, the other two the garden. There is also a villa at the back of the garden, which has two flats. This villa always seems to be in the shade, surrounded by trees. Palisady 51 itself and the front garden are fenced in with high iron railings and there are big ornate gates. The path from these gates is paved; on either side there are rose beds. In the winter these standard roses are wrapped in straw and sacking. No one steps on the lawn, of course. Just before the six wide steps, which lead into the entrance hall, a narrow path leads to the right of the concierge's flat. You have to descend six steps to their front door. On the left side are small windows providing light to the basement laundry.

Once you ascend those six steps you are in the open entrance lobby. The floor is a mosaic depicting a mythological scene, surrounded by garlands of roses and laurel. Facing the steps are half-glazed double doors leading to the garden, on the right, two steps lead up to the apartment in which Aunt Janka lived. To the left are heavy wooden double doors leading into the building itself. Just inside these doors, on the right, are steps leading into the cellars. Then there are three steps up to the doors to the ground floor – or rather mezzanine – apartments and to the main stone staircase, with its convoluted wrought iron banisters curved in a semi-circle from floor to floor. On floor one, on the left, there are two doors at right angles to each other; on the second floor there is only one door on the left and one on the right - our apartment. There is also an iron door in the centre leading up to the attics and, beside our door, a smaller one leads up to other storerooms. The staircase forms the centre of the house. There are twenty-seven steps between every storey; seventeen down to the cellars and twenty up into the attics.

It was normal for people residing in a town to live in apartments, only very few people had a 'family house'. Naturally, apartments varied enormously but they all had one thing in common: none had bespoke laundry facilities – unless you counted the cold water tap in the kitchen or the bath and basin in the bathroom. Therefore, the wash was done in the communal laundry rooms in the cellar.

At the end of each year, the concierge brought the new calendar to the owners of the apartments. It went by seniority; the longer you had lived there, the sooner you got it and that meant that the first people had most choices of washing days. Initially, you could only put down one day a month but, after everyone had had their first option, the calendar went round a second and sometimes even a third. That meant, if you were lucky, that occasionally you could get two days together but there was a long debate on whether that was better than having a second 'small' washday a fortnight after the big one. Obviously, everybody wanted to wash on a Monday but there were eight apartments and no months with eight Mondays. Christmas and Easter brought additional problems. So it was taken for granted that you would be 'reasonable'. Reasonableness caused more aggravation and quarrels than anything else. Fortunately, my Aunt Janka lived in the same building, so mother and she became an unholy alliance in respect of the laundry.

By the time I was seven, we had lived at the Palisades for four years and were, if not the oldest inhabitants - a couple of old ladies living across the landing from us had that privilege - nevertheless well up the tree of preference. I can remember well the joyous day, when Mother received a pristine calendar for the first time and had first choice. Washday was a big occasion. Smalls, ladies underwear, blouses and stockings, were washed in the bathroom as and when needed and suspended on a line over the bath. That did not count as real laundry. Bedding was linen or cotton, father's shirts were cotton and silk (silk shirts went to the professional laundry), nighties were cotton in the summer and flannel in the winter, table linen was always white damask, towels were white huckaback or terry – there was always a lot of washing to be done. There was no place in the apartment to store dirty washing. It was put into a basket in our local section of the attic. On the appointed Monday the washerwoman, Anna, came early in the morning, never later than six o'clock. Before she had even arrived, the boiler in the basement laundry had been filled and lit.

Anna was a big, hefty woman. Her hair was a sort of mousy colour and when she arrived her long plait was twisted up at the back of her head and held in place with big hairpins. As the day wore on, the pins became fewer and fewer and at the end of it, the plait hung down her back and little wisps of damp curling hair surrounded her jolly face. I thought that she looked much nicer then. She wore peasant dress; a full skirt, white blouse with wide sleeves, an apron of a flowered material and a waistcoat laced up the front. Over it all was a big shawl, crossed over in front and tied at the back, except when the weather was really hot. The shawl apron and waistcoat were discarded while she washed and the sleeves were rolled up above the elbows.

Anna came with a big basket over her arm. The first thing she did was to take out a big sack from her basket and tie it round her middle. Her shawl, waistcoat and apron were folded up and put neatly in its place. Before she started to wash she had to have breakfast. It was acknowledged that washing was hard work and people who did hard work had to be well fed. Besides, a good washerwoman was worth her weight in gold so she had to be looked after well. Breakfast was invariably scrambled eggs made with six eggs and cream, some thick slices of ham, bread and butter and big cups of milky coffee. Washing made you thirsty and besides food, throughout the day, Anna was kept satiated with an unending supply of beer. Once breakfast was over, our maid and even the cook helped to carry the baskets of washing from the attic down to the cellar, all those ninety-one steps. Things like soap, both solid and liquid, and also soap shavings – the precursors of Lux flakes – home-made starch, boxes of soda crystals and blue squares, our own washing boards, brushes, pails, bowls large and small, wooden spoons, and wooden draining spoons had all been taken down even earlier. On the preceding Friday, the maid and anyone else who cared to help, had already reduced several bars of yellow soft soap into shavings.

As you came down the steps into the basement, there was a passage to the right and one to the left. The one on the right led to the individual coal cellars, each with a small wood-shuttered coal chute. The passage on the left led to the laundry room and then on to the individual keeping cellars where potatoes, carrots and other root vegetables were kept in the winter in wooden sand-filled boxes. Our bicycles were also stored there when not in use, as well as the sleigh, and anything else that had no place either in the apartment or the attic. The first space in the laundry was taken up by the big mangle. The laundry proper had two boilers, each in a corner. One was used to heat water for washing, the other to boil the whites, in a solution of soap shavings and soda. There were two cold-water taps with big zinc basins under them, two tables and two sets of trestles for the wooden washing troughs. A drain ran along the middle and at the back of the laundry. The trestles with the troughs sat astride this drain.

The Woman Without A Number

The normal procedure was for everything to be soaked in cold water to loosen the dirt; then to be washed in hot or cold water and soap in the troughs on the washboards with or without a brush and then, usually, boiled. Bed linen was not soaked in soda only in cold water before undergoing the same treatment and soda crystals were not added to things that had embroidery on them. Nighties were not boiled but I think practically everything else was. The washing was lifted out with the large draining spoons into pails, tipped into the troughs and then rinsed at least three times with cold water. The last cold rinse had some 'blue' put in it, to make it whiter.

In the meantime, cook had grated quantities of potatoes into cold water to produce starch, which was the white sediment. Gradually and carefully, boiling water was poured on it under constant stirring until a nearly transparent jelly-like substance was produced. This thick, warm mess was taken to the laundry where it was diluted, depending on the degree of stiffness needed. Aprons were the stiffest, so were shirt collars, then came table linen. Pillowcases were only lightly starched as were shirts and cotton nighties. Handkerchiefs and towels were not starched, but I am no longer certain about the other items. Just about everything we had was white, I never saw a coloured tablecloth or towel or handkerchief in all my childhood. 'You can see if something is clean or not if it's white' was the rule.

After the items had been rinsed and starched they were first wrung out by hand. Two pairs of hands were needed for towels, sheets or table linen; then off to the mangle. The bed of the mangle was large enough to take a double sheet folded down the middle. It must have been eight foot long and at least five foot wide and at each end there was a big round bar-handle. The top of the mangle, the frame, was weighted with a full-size millstone, held down by a wooden screw on three legs. You then pushed or pulled this contraption of wooden rollers along the full length of the base. That was slightly on a slant and at the lower end there was a drain. The washed item was laid flat on the lower bed and as the frame was pushed over it, water was squeezed out and ran into the gutter. The frame was rolled back, the laundry carefully lifted off the bed, folded and placed in a basket to be taken and hung up to dry in the attic.

Throughout the day the washerwoman was fed. Mid-morning break was bread and butter and cheese and several glasses of milk; lunch started naturally with soup – leek and potato or beans – something filling, then a big steak with fried potatoes and finally pancakes. In the afternoon, it was yeast cakes and coffee and when she finished, she had another steak or half a roast chicken with more fried potatoes. Food for us on washday was a different matter, there was little time for cook to prepare anything. We all had a dish I loathed, consisting of Savoy cabbage and potatoes cooked with caraway seeds into a thick soup. The smell, added to the odour of wet washing, because usually the opportunity was taken to wash 'smalls' in the bathroom on washday, permeated the apartment and greeted me when I came home from school to have lunch long before I even reached our front door. It was the one thing I refused to eat, even if it meant having just dry bread.

Next in the washday routine, the baskets of wet laundry were taken up to the attic, where each apartment had a large cage. Part of it had ropes stretched across. If one was careful when taking wet washing out and hanging it up, it would dry with few creases and so make ironing easier. Anna stayed overnight when it was a really big wash which took two full days when everything, including sheets, pillowcases, duvet covers, featherbed covers, towels, tea

215

towels, table clothes, napkins, dust sheets which covered the furniture and net curtains were tackled. A truckle bed was opened up in the kitchen as it was too far for her to go back to Topolcianky, where she normally lived. Grandmother had come from nearby Topolciany, Topol's place, which was a sizeable village some distance from Bratislava, big enough to have a school. Topolcianky, Topol's little place, was where all our cooks and maids came from. While with us they always found boyfriends, young men working for the baker, the butcher, the greengrocer, postman or one of the soldiers stationed at the castle at the top of the hill. When they got married, they sent their younger sister or a cousin to take their place.

After washing came the ironing. The ironing woman was exactly the opposite of the washerwoman. Where the latter was wide the former was thin, where the latter was dumpy the former was lanky, the only strength she had was in her arms. Ironing also upset the normal routine of our meals. Again, priority had to be given to the incoming worker. Ironing is thirsty work, so the woman had a continuous supply of freshly made lemonade, flagons of soda water and a drink I found horrible – milk mixed with soda water. In respect of food, soups were the order of the day. Exquisite chicken soup with homemade pasta or tomato consommé with croutons, or cream of cauliflower soup were followed by a fruit compote, as became a worker with strong hands but a delicate stomach.

Usually, it took a week for the washing to dry. On the following Monday, the ironing woman came. The washing was brought down from the attic in big, square, two-handled wicker baskets. The dry washing was then sprinkled with water and rolled up to dampen it because it had become too dry for ironing and linen and cotton could not be ironed dry. After a sheet had been sprinkled, it had to be pulled and folded. Pulling was great fun and I was allowed to help when I got bigger because for large items you could use four people but most could be pulled by two. You stood facing each other and each person took two corners. You backed away from each other until the item was flat between you. It was then pulled first crosswise several times, then lengthwise by gathering the folds in each hand and pulling hard in a sawing fashion. Then you pulled your hands apart and between you the item was folded into a neat shape.

While the washing got to the required state of dampness, the irons were prepared. Initially, they were filled with charcoal. That was set alight and, in order to speed up heating, the maid took the iron on to the landing and swung it round and round until the charcoal was red and glowing. The iron was then taken to the ironing woman who would test it on a piece of brown paper to see whether it had reached the right temperature. While one iron was being used, the next one was set up and then a third. When the first one had cooled down it was taken to be swung around again and to have more charcoal added to it, if necessary. It was all very hard work. There was no ironing board but a kitchen table with layers of blankets and an old sheet on top sufficed. The pillowcases had frills around them and could not be ironed on the table. For this we had a goffering stand; a rounded brass rod on a stand and the frills were taken around it while being ironed. It was also used for the tops of gathered sleeves, particularly on the white aprons I wore to school.

There were always stacks of pink tissue paper. These were used to make the linen look pretty. As the sheets and pillowcases were folded a freshly pressed pink sheet was inserted in the top fold, so that a slight pink tinge was visible. The linen was kept in a press in my parents' bedroom. These shelves were covered with linen strips with a wide crocheted lace edging. It was a job my mother always did herself, no one else could stack as neatly as she did. Mother insisted on proper rotation, so every time it was all hands on deck to hold piles of linen while the freshly washed stuff was placed on the bottom. You almost felt guilty when clean bed linen was taken out, the pink tissue being carefully removed for re-use.

OUR FAMILY WAS NOT a conventional one. Grandfather was a larger than life, slightly eccentric character but the really odd one out was Mother, who was way ahead of her time. She had no desire to become a housewife and mother although she had no objection to the status of a married woman. During the First World War she had learned shorthand and typing and at the end of it she was, unusually, a female clerk of the court. It was useful after the war, when inflation was so great that she was paid twice a day, midday and in the evening, as the value of the money was changing so swiftly. At midday she took a large shopping bag full of money to the baker to get a loaf of bread. By the evening that money would not have even paid for a crust. I can remember Grandfather saying that it had been cheaper to paper the walls with money than with wallpaper and that is what he actually had done.

Father was born in 1886 in Hungary and was the youngest of four children; his father had a bookshop in a small place in Hungary called Pincehely. Father was sent to the grammar school at the nearest bigger town, Bonyhád and dreamt of becoming a doctor. But he was the right age to be called up in 1914. He became an officer and an official photographer in the Hungarian Army.

After the war, by which time his two sisters Teresa and

Bella had married, it was decided that father's elder brother, who was also married and who had a young son, should go to the States to make his fortune and hopefully that of the family. His little son stayed behind with Grandmother and my father paid for his education. When he had completed it, he was sent to join his parents. But they never became rich. The son became a teacher. I found his address after the Second World War, by which time he had retired. We kept in touch for a few years. I think he must have died, because my last Christmas card in the early 1950's was returned, addressee unknown.

Father's dream to study medicine was not possible, as he had to support his mother and nephew, instead he went into insurance and in 1922 became the area manager of the Assicuriazioni Generali of Trieste in Kosice, a town in Eastern Slovakia. He and my Mother married in 1922 and they went to live in Kosice and that was where I was born in November 1923. My maternal grandfather's health deteriorated and, having no sons, he looked to his son-in-law to carry on their business; knowing full well that his eldest daughter, my mother, was going to be the one who wore the trousers, at least as far as the business was concerned. The family moved to Bratislava, Father taking over the branch of the insurance company there and Mother running the business. I was told that she was the first woman in Czechoslovakia to obtain a driving licence, but she was a menace on the road and Father would not allow her to drive if he or any of the children were with her.

By the time my brother, Tomy, was born in 1929, Father had left the insurance company and become a partner in grandfather's business, which then moved to bigger premises and also started to deal wholesale in bicycles, sewing machines, prams and also eventually gramophones and wirelesses. We were keeping up with the times and new

technology. The young men from the villages would first of
all buy a bicycle on the never-never, we did our own finance
arrangements, repaying the debt over a period of ten years.
During this time they would invariably meet a girl. She
would need a sewing machine to prepare her trousseau, also
on the never-never, repaid over twenty-five years and then
the baby would come along, which needed a pram and then
a pushchair and eventually they would have quiet evenings
listening to the gramophone or wireless. So, all their needs
were taken care of in one place. It could not fail and it didn't,
the business flourished. Elbogen & Kaufmann were
plastered in gold letters on a bright blue background - I had
been allowed by Grandfather to choose them - spread across
the three big windows of the shop.

UNTIL I WAS ABOUT nine, Grandma and Grandfather
lived in the very centre of the town. The house fronted onto
the market square. It was a big house with wide wooden
gates one half of which was permanently closed and in the
other half there was a door. You had to step over a high
threshold to get through the door. The gateway must have
been at least twenty feet long, it was really a cobbled tunnel
going under the front half of the house and leading to a big
cobbled yard. On the ground floor, where once there must
have been stables, were big doorways leading to places
which I never managed to explore.

The house was really a hollow square, with walkways on
each of the three floors and stairs going up each side, but
inside the building. The half of the gateway which was closed,
for its full length, was a workshop. The staircases at the front
and at the back were quite grand affairs with wrought iron
railings but the two side ones were narrower and dark and
were only used by the maids, cooks and the postman.

I was proudly told that in the closed-off section of the gateway Grandfather had laid the foundations of the business after the First World War by making and repairing penny-farthing bicycles and also the odd sewing machine. Now there was a cobbler there. Grandfather's business had grown and was now in its second home, on a prime site on Commercial Street. It was moved from there, when I was about 12, to the 'Passage', an arcade of shops that were the pre-cursor of the covered shopping precinct. Since we lived in times when you got a guarantee for ten years when buying a bike, or twenty-five if buying a sewing machine, spare parts for all the goods sold had to be kept; gramophone and sewing machine needles, tyres for bicycles and prams, 'dry' batteries and carbide for bicycle lamps, links for repairing bicycle chains and pretty nets to cover the rear wheels of ladies bikes so that skirts would not get tangled up in the spokes.

There were two apartments each side of the house on every floor, a total of eight per floor. Those at the front and the back were superior and had windows onto the street as well as the walkways but those on the side only had windows to the walkways. The front of the house was deemed to be the premier position, except on the market square, because there you had all the noise and dust of the market. The back apartments had windows that looked out onto a quiet side street.

The first floor was the best one, especially as there were no lifts and everything had to be carried up the stairs. The size of the apartments varied. It was quite normal that if a family grew and the people next door were willing, one or more of the adjacent rooms were sold off and connecting doors built with the previous ones bricked up. There was no telling how large an apartment was from the outside.

Grandma's apartment was on the first floor at the back. In

front of it, in the summer, like most others, there was a riot of red geraniums and carnations in pots. I can remember the hall, the kitchen, a sitting room from which, I think, opened the bedroom. There must have been other rooms because I had dinner there at midday always at the dining table once I started school and the maid must also have lived somewhere. If you wanted to go to the toilet, you had to go out of the front door and next to it was the one to the toilet. This was lucky as not every apartment had a toilet so conveniently placed. The bathroom was off the bedroom and was always cold.

My seventh birthday was on the same day as the seventieth of my Aunt Josephine, the eldest sister of Grandmother, so it was decided that there would be a joint celebration even though we shared little in common. Aunt Josephine was a small, bird-like woman. She was widowed and lived in a home for elderly ladies where she had her own furniture in her room and did not have to worry about finding servants to do her cooking or washing. I can only remember that it was very difficult to move in her room on account of all the furniture. The birthday party was to be at Grandma's and all the family were naturally invited. My brother Tomy was still a baby – six years younger that I – and on this occasion I cannot remember him being there, so he might have been at home with nanny, 'Fraulein'.

I can vividly remember all the red plush drawing room furniture and in particular, the white antimacassars on the sofa on which Aunt Josephine sat in state and where I was also supposed to sit to receive the wishes - and presents – of the guests. I didn't see Aunt Josephine very often, I did not like her smell, she used a particularly sweet scent and she did not seem to like me much either. It was evening and dark when my parents and I walked home.

As children do I asked innocently, 'Why doesn't Aunt Josephine like me?'

'Whoever said she didn't?' asked Mother.

'No-one but she is sort of different to me.'

'She's afraid of you!' burst in Father with a laugh.

'Afraid? But she is bigger than I am.'

'Ben', warned my mother, 'there is really no need to …'

'No need for what?' I persisted.

It was exactly the wrong strategy to get me away from the subject. I would now keep on and on, until, in exasperation, I was told something. I don't think I have changed much in that respect.

'You'll know tomorrow,' promised Father.

He got such a look from Mother, I knew he would be in trouble once she got him on her own. But Father could cope, he was the only one who really could; he could laugh Mother out of her most paprika moods.

Next day, it must have been Sunday, Father went to play chess at the Astoria coffee house and, as he had started to teach me the game, I was allowed to accompany him and *kibbitz* (watch), provided I never opened my mouth. It was difficult but watching chess was worth it. On this particular day, he dropped me at Grandma's so that she should tell me why Aunt Josephine was afraid of me. That way Mother could not possibly object to my finding out. The explanation was forthcoming. When I was about six weeks old, my parents brought me from Kosice to Bratislava to show me off to all the family. Naturally, the family get-together was at Grandma's. In those days babies were swaddled. They were laid on a long bolster which was folded over so that just the head and arms were outside and then the whole thing was wrapped over and over with ribbons, until it became a manageable parcel to carry. Babies were kept swaddled nearly all the time and were also transported in this way.

So there I was, in all my glory, displayed on the settee, for everyone to admire and for the ladies of the family to pick up and coo over. Aunt Josephine never had any children and she was always a great 'cooer' over babies. Being the eldest in the family, she was the first one to pick me up, bringing me close to her face. Being even then an inquisitive child, I stretched out my hands to touch Aunt Josephine's beautifully coiffured white hair and with one twist of the wrist I had it in my hands and tried to stuff it into my mouth. No one had suspected that Aunt Josephine wore a wig and was all but bald.

She threw me onto the settee, grabbed her wig, shrieking, 'This is not a child, but a devil!' She never liked me after that.

I WAS THREE YEARS old when Aunt Janka got married. It was going to be a very special wedding that would take place in Uncle Béla's magnificent house in Vienna and I was to be a bridesmaid. Uncle Béla was one of Grandmother's brothers. They were a very big family; Great-grandmother had, it was said, eighteen children of whom eleven survived to adulthood which was quite an achievement for the middle of the nineteenth century. The age gap between the eldest and the youngest was more than twenty years which created quite a lot of muddle in my family. My mother's best friend, who was at least ten years younger than she was, was Edith, who was really her aunt and I spent a lot of my early childhood playing with Gertie, Edith's sister, who was only a month older than me. We considered ourselves cousins, although she really was my aunt. Grandmother had two daughters, Irene, my mother and her younger sister Janka. But grandmother had so many siblings there was no need to have many children each to make us a big extended family.

Uncle Béla was always a mystery figure to me. He was the rich Uncle who lived in this big house in Vienna. From snippets of information and using my imagination, I concocted his history. I never had the opportunity to find out in later years how much was fact and how much of it fruits of my fertile invention. Uncle Béla had previously had contacts with China, he was then president and owner of a big paper and pulp company with offices, besides Vienna, in Amsterdam, Sydney, Shanghai and New York. That was fact and there might even have been more of them. He was the one to whom everybody in the family turned if they needed financial help, a job or advice. And from what I heard later, he never said no. You might not get exactly what you asked for, but he looked after the family.

Aunt Janka was really beautiful. She had Grandmother's sparkling auburn, nearly titian-red hair, huge dark eyes, a perfect oval face and a willowy figure. The groom was apparently quite a catch, a solicitor, with a big estate encompassing several farms, vineyards and a tobacco plantation, on the eastern border between Hungary and Slovakia. So no ordinary wedding would do. Grandmother went to Vienna and consulted Uncle Béla. He seemed impressed and offered his house for the wedding. He was going to host the whole do and no half-measures. Janka should have a send-off that would be remembered for a long time and the whole family would gather in Vienna for this wedding of weddings.

Naturally, there were problems. To start with, the wedding presents. They were normally displayed at the reception, so one had to make certain that whatever was given was just that bit better or dearer than was expected. Of course, the bride would have her trousseau, just as I had twenty years later although by then it was no longer usual. My parents decided that they would provide all the bed linen. It would be hand-woven to order, the lace would be hand-made and the best seamstresses possible would do the embroidery. There would be 12 of everything: sheets, duvet covers, and large pillowcases, six for each person and a dozen small pillowcases for those pillows you stuffed under your neck. Because it had to be displayed, it had to be taken to Vienna before the wedding. Each piece had been carefully pressed while still damp and the pillowcases lightly starched, so that they were smooth and glistening. Into each piece of linen a sheet of pink tissue paper had been inserted under the embroidery and lace. Each piece was folded exactly in the same way, to the same size and wrapped in white tissue paper and then the whole lot was divided into six parcels and each was placed in a white linen bag for the journey to Vienna. It would look a splendid present.

At that time there was a border between Austria and Czechoslovakia and you were not supposed to take new goods out of one country and into another without paying customs duty. This created a problem, after all, these things were not going to stay in Vienna, they were only going to be shown off at the reception. The bride and groom were allowed to bring their presents back with them, that was a concession given to all new couples who married abroad. Grandmother thought that she could wrap some of the sheets round her middle and be just a very fat lady for a couple of trips to Vienna. Mother thought that this might also be possible with the duvet covers, if they got creased it was not difficult to press them again in Vienna but the pillowcases created a problem. They could not possibly be opened out and wrapped round people; they had to stay in their nice smart shape.

I was asked to help. I was always a very truthful child, mainly because I could not remember if I told a lie what I had said. I have learned to be economical with the truth, by not telling everything but I still do not tell lies. In those days trains had carriages in three classes. First class was something very special and we would not have thought of travelling in it. Second was how we usually travelled which was quite comfortable but third only had wooden slatted benches, like those in the park and could be quite painful to small bottoms. It was decided that, on this occasion, we would travel third class and the pillows would be camouflaged as a cushion for me to sit on but just for during the period we went through customs. Off we went, Grandmother, Mother and I with a big parcel wrapped in a coloured cloth. We were fortunate, it was midweek and no one shared our carriage.

Just before the train stopped at the border and the customs officer came on board, the parcel was lifted down and I was sat on it. The instructions were that I must on no account open my mouth to say anything while the customs officer inspected our passports and looked at the luggage and, especially, nothing about what I was sitting on.

I was always a chatty child and to be quiet when someone came into our carriage was really difficult for me, particularly when the customs officer remarked, 'How right of you to bring a cushion for the little one to sit on, those seats are not at all comfortable.'

Although our cases were opened, they never thought of asking me to get off the cushion to inspect it. I was dying to tell them that it wasn't really a cushion but Aunt Janka's wedding present and that I was helping mother to get them to Vienna. Mother and Grandmother heaved a sigh of relief when the train started again.

I cannot remember anything about the actual wedding even though I was one of the bridesmaids. What I do recall is being in this big room afterwards, with lots of windows that opened out onto the gardens. Some had window-seats. I was sitting on one, half hidden by the curtains, and it was dusk. There were a lot of people in the room and I liked it that it was getting dark outside and that I was neither in the room with the people nor outside in the garden. Later, when it was dark, my parents, grandparents and I went by taxi to the station to catch the train back to Bratislava. It was raining and dark. I was sitting on my Father's lap beside the driver and Mother and Grandma and Grandpa were in the back. And then there was a crash and glass splintering into my eyes and I heard myself scream. I remember being in the hospital; everything was white except for the bottom part of the walls and those were deep green and I was sitting on a table swinging my legs but with mother's handkerchief over my eye while Father looked very concerned.

I had to have several stitches above my left eye and they worried whether I would lose the sight in it. I don't remember when the bandages were changed and I could, in theory, open both eyes again but I could not open my left eye very well and Mother was saying, 'If the scar stays and gets ugly, we can always get a cosmetic done on it.'

The scar went through my left eyelid and eyebrow, except that they must have shaved it off, because I remember it growing back, except in one place, where a piece of the eyebrow was missing for many years. The scar looked like an up-turned chair and I was certain that it would be all right because Mother could get a cosmetic done on it; whatever that meant.

The scar faded, the hair in my eyebrow grew over it and by the time I was fifteen or so, I knew what a cosmetic was and I wasn't keen to have one done on my left eyebrow. I was much more pre-occupied with my nose, which I thought far too big.

13

*

Assorted Characters

I was the eldest granddaughter, the first grandchild and my grandfather adored me. From the beginning I was treated by him not as a child, but as a lady. Yet he supported my tomboyish escapades. I really did not want to be a girl at all and I told him so often, except on my birthday, on account of his birthday presents.

My name was of the period, that of a flower. It sounds much nicer in Hungarian than in English; my proper name, Ibolyka, got abbreviated by me, who could not pronounce it, into Ibi, or as I later spelled it Iby. My birthday was at the end of November and when I was a child there were no hothouse flowers in the winter; to get even a single red carnation was deemed absolute extravagance. On my birthday, Grandfather always gave me a little basket filled with as many bunches of Parma violets as my age. Underneath the flowers there was always a hidden grown-up present. Sometimes a small bottle of perfume, a silver ring or a locket for my necklace and, when I was eight and could really tell the time, a beautiful silver watch on a silver bracelet. Mother used to shake her head and proposed that I should put these presents away until I was older and could appreciate them better but I was allowed to wear or use the presents on those days when I was not at school.

There was a story my Grandfather used to tell about me and my liking of meat. I was about three and spending the day with Grandmother. I had had, as was usual, my lunch in the kitchen and was swinging my legs as high as possible to see how often I could hit the underside of the big, white-scrubbed wooden table, just strong enough for me to know that I had hit it but not so brashly as to make a noise so that I would be reprimanded. It took very delicate judgement and concentration and was better done when one did not try to take a mouthful of food at the same time, so it took me rather a long time to eat my lunch. In any case, salt and spices were not included in children's food, it was always bland and uninteresting.

I had finished lunch by the time Grandfather came home for his. Naturally, he had it in the dining room and I was allowed to accompany him, watch him open out the big, white, starched napkin, tuck it into his collar and sit back and await the arrival of the dishes. Soup was normal and I had had some as well but the next dish puzzled me:

'Grandfather, what is that black thing?'

'Meat, steak,' he told me.

'What's steak? I never get food that colour. Mine is always sort of white.'

For children chicken and perhaps braised veal was deemed appropriate, not a big seared, bloody steak.

'Grandfather, can I taste?' I asked.

Grandmother objected. It was not fit food for a child but Grandfather prevailed.

'A mouthful won't do her any harm,' he decreed. 'You always say she is anaemic, it will do her good.'

So a small piece from the black edge was cut off and handed to me by Grandfather on the tip of his fork and I loved it.

'Oh, grandfather, I do like this food. Can I have some more, please?'

But then Grandmother put her foot down. She was good at it, nearly as good as Mother. It was not good for me, Mother would have to give permission, I shouldn't get tit-bits from the table, I wasn't a pet dog. In disgrace and snuffling audibly I went to the kitchen, where I knew I would always get sympathy from cook and usually something sweet to nibble, even if only a couple of raisins.

Somewhat later that day, after Grandfather had had his after-lunch snooze, he told me not to be upset, he would see to things. He was good at seeing to things, just as good as Grandmother was at putting her foot down.

The next morning Grandfather decided to take me out for a ride. He always rode in a Fiaker [Hackney cab], he did not believe in cars and the thought of riding in a tram or bus would never have entered his mind. An outing in a Fiaker was a real treat for me. I did not really like horses, they were too big and smelly and farted, but the inside of the Fiaker smelled of leather and of Grandfather's cigars. It was a beautiful morning, so the top was put down and I sat proudly opposite Grandfather. Grandmother had decided that if I were to spend the morning with Grandfather, she would go visiting. Strict instructions were left that I had to be back by midday and for cook to prepare my lunch for that time.

We drove through town, many gentlemen doffed their hats to Grandfather and he inclined his head, sometimes even took out his cigar and on a few occasions raised his hat as well and I kept asking who was who. We stopped on the way at the butcher's. The driver got off his high seat, had a whispered conversation with Grandfather, went into the shop and came back a few minutes later with a parcel.

Grandfather asked, 'You got exactly what I said?'

'But of course, sir,' he demurely replied.

'What is in that parcel?' I asked.

'Hmm, what do you get from a butcher?' asked Grandfather.

'Just meat,' I replied.

'So why ask?' was the terse reply.

I was puzzled. Grandmother usually went shopping with cook to the market and I knew that she always brought all the food home. So why was Grandfather getting meat? But he had been a bit short, so I thought it better not to ask questions for a couple of minutes.

When we got back home, Grandfather picked up the parcel and we went upstairs. He rang the bell with the silver top of his stick. Cook opened the door.

'Oh, you're just in time. I got your lunch all ready,' cook said to me.

'There's no hurry,' said Grandfather. 'I think it would be a nice change for the child to have this for her lunch. When it is ready, let us know, we'll be in the study.'

In there, Grandfather sat down to read the paper and told me to be quiet and look at some picture books. I was getting hungry, it was past my lunchtime.

About half an hour later, cook came in to tell us that my lunch was ready. I got up to go with her. Grandfather also got up and said he would come with me. That was unusual, he did not belong in the kitchen.

I sat down on my usual chair with the two cushions on it so that I could reach up to the tabletop and cook put in front of me, not my usual little plate, but a large dish with a steak on it.

Her face was disapproving, to put it mildly.

'But it's black, it's meat, real meat,' I warbled joyously.

'Yes,' said Grandfather. 'Enjoy it.'

According to Grandfather I ate the whole one-pound fillet. I remember that when I got back home, I often asked for black, real meat but rarely got it and Grandfather spread the news all over town that he had a four-year-old Granddaughter who could eat a pound of steak at a single sitting.

IN ALL BLOCKS OF apartments, the concierge locked the gates at ten at night and opened them again at five o'clock in the morning. All residents had keys but not the servants, they had to be in before ten even on their day off. If you forgot the key you had to ring the bell for the concierge. He was never pleased to open the gate and you had to pay him for doing so. This system was supposed to keep out burglars, nevertheless adults seemed to live in fear of them.

Banks were not used as today, there were no 'holes in the wall' where one could deposit the day's takings after the banks had closed, all business was undertaken in cash. In that era, the difference between a retail and a wholesale shop was not clearly defined. We were wholesalers to many small businesses because, being a big one, we could negotiate special terms and prices with the manufacturers and the same applied to spare parts. We lived at a time when everything was repaired and patched and mended, when no one would dream of going off on the bike without a puncture repair kit.

There was also a workshop in which the bicycles were originally repaired, which was the origin of the little business empire. Grandfather would not have countenanced the discontinuation of it under any circumstances even when, having retired, and the business no longer being 'Elbogen' became 'Elbogen & Kaufmann.'

233

The Woman Without A Number

Bills to the factories were paid by credit transfer through the bank, wages and salaries in cash and the takings were brought home. By the end of the week, even if wages and everything possible had been taken out, there was still a lot left, especially if the owners of the little shops had been in and paid up. The money was hidden in all sorts of places, Mother was expert in finding new hiding holes but, nevertheless, the apartment was never left empty at night.

As an officer in the reserve of the Hungarian Army, Father had his service revolver at home. His batman came from the village once a week, checked that Father could still get into his uniform, brushed it and shined the boots and, I presume, cleaned the gun. I was never allowed to be present when anything like that took place and both cook and the maid had to be in together, because the batman had a reputation of having an eye for the ladies and, according to what I overheard, could not be trusted with simple, honest and trusting girls. He certainly would not have been allowed to 'call' on the girls.

Father's gun was kept in a locked drawer in his bedside cabinet – in case of burglars.

It was a Saturday night, I had gone to sleep a long time beforehand and my parents had been out dancing, they were crazy about it and my Mother's dance frocks with handkerchief point skirts in flowered chiffon with floating bits here and there were, to me, something suitable for angels in heaven. I heard them come in. They locked up and went to bed. Everything was quiet.

All of a sudden there was a sharp noise and then I heard a shot, glass breaking and someone screaming. I flew out of my bed: a burglar! We were having a burglary, how exciting. Had Father shot him? Where was he? He could not have jumped out of the window, after all we were on the second floor, in which case he must be dead. I ran into the living

234

room. There was mother in her long white nightie, both maids similarly attired, as well as Father who was holding his hand and dripping blood all over the place. Father had been shot! Mother shouted for me to go back to bed, something I certainly could not do with all the excitement going on and the screaming and shouting and I was bursting again with questions. It was obvious that no one had time to answer, so I did not ask them.

'Water, water,' my mother called. One of the maids rushed in with a bowl.

'A towel, get a towel, a clean one,' Mother shouted. Cook brought a white towel. Father put his hand into the bowl and all the water promptly turned red, I thought he was bleeding to death. Cook screamed. The maid screamed. Mother screamed. I didn't scream, I just fainted. Not for long, though, just enough to add to the pandemonium.

When I came to I was on a chair, supported by cook, Father had his hand wrapped up in the towel and was sitting on another chair supported by Mother. The maid had been sent to fetch the doctor as we did not have a telephone at home. He came very quickly. After inspecting Father's hand, he shook his head and said, 'You have to go to the hospital to have some stitches put in. I'll take you, I've got my carriage. How did you do this? Your gun? That's no bullet wound.'

Father explained.

'Hmm, that gun of yours has a nasty recoil,' said the Doctor. 'When was it cleaned last?'

So it wasn't the burglar who had been doing the shooting, it was Father who had shot the burglar. But where was he? Was he lying somewhere dead and no one was taking any notice of him? Perhaps in Father's study? Or had he escaped? Had he jumped from the window? What had he taken?

The Woman Without A Number

Mother thought that I was getting overexcited and the doctor agreed. I was given a few drops of something on a lump of sugar to make me sleep and it must have done the trick because the next thing I knew was that it was morning. Naturally, then I wanted to know where the burglar was. I was told there had been no burglary. Evidently, a small picture had fallen from the wall in the sitting room. Half asleep, Father heard the crash, thought there was a burglar in the apartment, fumbled for the gun, rushed into the sitting room and fired out of the window to scare the perpetrator away.

One of the double windows had to have a new pane in it, it was very big and cost a lot of money. The fine pleated voile curtains had a nasty hole in them and were carefully repaired but I always knew where the hole had been. Fortunately, that was the only burglary we never had.

Mother asked Father never, ever to use the gun again and it was locked up in a chest in the attic. Instead, he put his sword under the bed, should a burglar come for real. Father had to have four stitches in his hand, had it bandaged up for quite a long time, had to answer some awkward questions from his chess-playing pals, couldn't play the violin for ages and I was told never to tell anyone that father got hurt while trying to shoot a non-existent burglar.

I NEVER KNEW WHAT my Mother's hobbies were; she was always too busy and she only indulged in them after she retired. Father had a more relaxed attitude to life and he made no secrets of his, they were very apparent. On Sunday afternoons he took part in regular chess tournaments and he also taught me to play the game. He said it would help me to think clearly. He played the violin well and had, what I believed to be, a Stradivarius. It was lost in the war and I never found out whether the yellowing label inside the instrument indicated a copy or the real thing. On Sunday evenings, chamber music was a regular occurrence. When I became old and proficient enough on the piano, I joined them and then the quartet became a piano quintet.

From his youth, Father had been an ardent photographer and I think that he considered that really his prime hobby and now that we had a car, he could take pictures in more and more exciting places. In those days photography was not a 'point and click' affair. It needed not only a big, delicate camera but also plates instead of film, a tripod, a black cloth cover, magnesium flares as flash guns and lots of other things – collectively referred to by us as 'the paraphernalia'. Wherever we went by car, the paraphernalia came too.

I can remember many times, when a child, being allowed to look through the albums in which Father had collected the photos he took during the First World War. I asked him whether he had ever had any time to do any fighting. He used to smile and say, 'Not really, because I was an official photographer. But these are the pictures I took for myself.'

Some of them I considered very funny, like the one where the Chiefs of Staff of the Hungarian army were sitting on the field latrine, actually just a tree trunk over a pit, surrounded by screens, with their trousers around their ankles, jackets unbuttoned, but with cigars in their hands. I think Father must have had a judicious hole-in-the-wall somewhere.

One photo was of officers, ladies and children sitting out of doors at a large beautifully laid table, with Father at the head of it, celebrating the Emperor's birthday. There was another of an old-fashioned lorry with soldiers waving from the back, of someone cranking the engine of a military car, sleeves rolled up, with coat and cap draped over the bonnet and snow all around. Another of an aeroplane and an airman reaching out and lobbing grenades from the planes, people running in all directions, into tents, into ditches, campstools overturned. I wondered how Father managed to have his tripod and paraphernalia in the right place at the right time.

Until 1919, the Czech Republic, Slovak Republic, Northern Italy, Austria and Hungary had all been part of the Hapsburg Empire and, as a result, there were members of our family scattered across these countries. Visiting family and friends could be quite difficult because of the border formalities, passports and even visas needed, although the train to Vienna took only an hour. To visit the zoo at Schönbrunn would certainly be not much more than an hour in the new Ford that Father bought in about 1930.

It was a lovely day. First of all, we visited Uncle Béla and his family in Vienna and showed off the car. After it was duly admired – not many people had cars in those days – Father said that he had promised to take me to the zoo and that we would be back for afternoon coffee and cakes later. It was a lovely summer day and Father was keen to get photos of Mother and me and my baby brother with as many animals as possible. Eventually Mother asked, 'Just for a change, can't we have just one photo of ourselves, without animals? What about here, in front of these lovely flowers?'

'Yes,' said Father, 'that's an excellent idea. You can hold the little monkey in your arms.' In Hungarian the term 'little monkey' is a nickname for a baby and my brother, who had inherited my Mother's olive skin and jet-black hair, looked to my imaginative eyes really like some of the little monkeys we had been looking at.

Father set up the tripod near to an enclosure and we posed in front of the flowerbed.

'Can't you go back a little further? I can't get your feet in,' he queried.

We moved back as far as possible. The flowerbed was

surrounded by a low barrier of metal hoops and a big notice warned us not to step on to it or even go on the grass, so we didn't.

Father said, 'That won't do. I'll just have to move the tripod.'

He moved it back about a foot, looked through the viewfinder, shook his head, lifted the tripod with the camera already fixed to it and kept on going backwards, looking through the viewfinder until the wire fence of an enclosure hit him on the back.

'This will have to do,' he said.

'But Daddy,' I said.

'But Ben,' Mother added.

Father was too busy to listen. He had to get the tripod just right, then he ducked under the black cloth and shouted, 'I shall count to three and when it comes to three, smile.'

'But Daddy,' I exclaimed.

'Ben, watch out,' Mother shouted.

'Quiet,' yelled Father from under the black cloth. 'I don't know how you expect a chap to concentrate and get a good picture, if you keep interrupting and can't be still and quiet.'

'Oh well,' sighed Mother.

From under the black cloth Father held up his left hand with the magnesium flare. He started to count, 'One, two, three.' At 'three' we smiled, the flash went off and the elephant standing behind the fence but very close to Father, wondering what this thing under the black cloth could be and raising his trunk to investigate further, took fright, turned his back on Father, trumpeted and started to pee. After all, it was the first time he had been confronted by a magnesium flare. Elephants are big animals and produce vast amounts of pee. Father got drenched but he held on to the tripod and camera, they were too precious and had to be protected as he tried to dodge the deluge. Mother and I were helpless.

'Don't just stand there laughing,' yelled Father, 'do something!'

'Oh, I can't,' gasped Mother between gusts of laughter, 'I've got to hold the little monkey!'

'Do something, Iby,' yelled Father.

'I c-c-c-c-c-can't,' I stuttered, 'It smells too much. I'll be sick.'

Eventually we calmed down somewhat, particularly as by now a large crowd was gathering around us to view the disaster area. Somehow, Father managed to unhook the sodden black cloth, fold the tripod and dismantle the camera. He squelched with us to the car park. Mother and I were keeping our distance and trying to disassociate ourselves from him. There, by the car, he had to strip completely, we refused point blank to let him into the car otherwise. He found a spare black cloth and wound it round his middle, Mother gave up her dustcoat, so that he should not be naked from the waist up, there was nothing we could do about shoes.

'What do I do with these things?' asked Father miserably, pointing at his clothes on the ground.

'I really don't care,' snapped Mother, 'but they are not coming into the car.'

'But it is my best summer suit' wailed Father.

'You mean it was. I don't think there is a cleaner in town who will touch it and I certainly won't have it in the house in its present state.' Mother could be very forceful.

A compromise was reached. The suit was wrapped in newspaper and put in the boot, which in our case was a separate suitcase-shaped box attached to the back of the car. This meant that room had to be found in the car for the camera and the paraphernalia. It also meant that we had to drive straight home. There was no chance now of having coffee and cakes at Uncle Béla's.

'All I hope,' said Mother tartly as we left Vienna behind

us, 'is that the customs people don't stop us at the border. I'd like to hear how you would explain why you are travelling in a skirt and a ladies coat and driving barefoot. Peed on by an elephant, indeed, I ask you – do you think they would believe you?'

'Oh yes, they would,' I piped up, 'If they looked in the boot.'

I LIKED SCHOOL. BECAUSE I was incurably inquisitive and drove parents, grandparents, nannies and domestics mad with my continuous questions, it suited me. Even when it came to bedtime stories I would not accept the 'and they lived happily ever after' formula. I wanted to know what happened next. I had been told that in school all your questions did get answered. I was very trusting but school produced a new problem for me, one I had not known existed; you see, I was left-handed.

Nobody had noticed anything odd at home. After all, at meal-times, being a well-brought up little girl, I ate with knife, fork and spoon as they were laid on the table and, being an only child until I was nearly six, I was in an environment devoid of other children and played on my own or, as I preferred, watched what the grown-ups did and tried to help.

I also went on long walks with the nanny, taking doll in the pram for an airing by the river or sometimes on the paddle steamer to the other side, where nanny or granny would have a rest on a bench in the shade, while I told my doll off. Doll did all those things I was dying to do, like climbing the walnut and the pear tree, playing in the sandpit after it had rained and the sand was all nice and squashy, picking the flowers off the runner beans after all, they were such a lovely red colour. How could I possibly know that those flowers would become long, stringy beans that were picked and shelled in the autumn and dried for the winter.

It did not take long for teacher to find out that I could not tell my right hand from my left one. When it came to writing, either would do for me but not for teacher.

'You have to use your right hand, the left hand is wrong,' she said.

'Why Miss?'

'Because all people write with the right hand.'

'Miss, which is my right hand?' I asked.

'The one you write with.'

'But I can write with both hands,' I said precociously

'No, you can't,' she insisted. 'All people write with their right hand only. You need the left hand to hold the slate.'

'But I can do that …'

'Don't argue, you are being disrespectful.'

'But Miss….'

'That's enough. Use the same hand as Olga!'

That made me angry, Olga again always Olga; teacher's pet, with curly, blond hair and plaits. I made a face behind teacher's back. It was a good thing she did not see it or it would have been the clapper for me, although girls only got the clapper very rarely, when teacher really lost her temper. Making faces at her made her really lose her temper.

A note was sent home, 'The child is disrespectful. Also she does not know which is her right hand.' That caused some consternation. I could draw equally well with either too. Father could not see any problem, nor did Mother really.

'Just use the right hand pet and then you won't get into trouble,' she advised.

'Which is my right hand?' I ventured.

'The one that holds the knife.'

Good, that made sense. Except that away from the table I could not remember in which hand I held the knife. My memory was excellent, but also very selective. So, in lesson, I just waited until Olga picked up the chalk or the pencil and followed, I had apparently 'learned' and after that the problem was solved.

Once a week, there were Physical Exercises and this always started with marching around in time with the clapper. The teacher called 'right turn' and all the class turned right, except for me, who waited to see which way Olga was turning. By the time I had and turned, I was overtaken by several children, had lost my place, tried to find it, and then teacher shouted 'left turn' and I got mixed up in another manoeuvre to regain my place and chaos ensued. Teacher yelled, 'Stop.'

She marched over to me and asked, in a not too friendly way and asked, 'And what were you doing? Why did you not turn right when everyone else did?'

'I did not know which was right,' I responded honestly.

'But you can write now with your right hand, can't you?'

'Well... I write with the same hand as Olga.'

'That is your right hand. Why can't you turn to the right?' Teacher went on.

'Because I can't remember which is my right hand.'

'You can't remember?' Her voice rose at least an octave.

'Well, I'll just have to help you remember!'

Fear struck into me. That was an ominous phrase, used to the boys before they got the clapper for cheeking or chatting but I had not done anything wrong. I could not help it if I could not remember which my right hand was.

'Please, Miss, not the clapper.' I wailed. The indignity of it, not to mention the indubitable pain if the howls of the boys were anything to go by. 'I really can't help it.'

'Oh, very well,' said teacher. 'Wait here everybody, not a whisper out of any of you. Any noise and you all get the clapper.'

The Woman Without A Number

The others were all giggling and pointing at me and I could have sunk into the floor with shame. To be different was bad enough but singled out could hardly be borne. Then teacher came back with a piece of red thread and tied it round my right wrist.

'Now I am putting this thread on your right hand,' she explained. 'Your right hand, child. You can see the red thread, can't you?'

'Yes Miss. Thank you Miss,' I replied, relieved.

'All right, class, off we go, in time with the clapper, turn left and trot. Left, right, left, right.

All the attention had got me confused. First I had to stop and check which was right and which was left. I lifted both my arms to see on which wrist was the red thread – now had teacher said it was on the right wrist or was it on the left one? Perhaps if I remembered in which hand I held my knife. I pretended to hold a knife in one hand and then in the other. Well, both were possible. The more children knocked into me, the more I got confused and in the end I turned, obviously in the wrong direction. Or rather, by the time I had worked out in which direction to turn, teacher had told the class to about turn.

That was at the beginning of the school year, in September. As the weather got colder, I started to wear long sleeves. Before each session of physical exercises teacher trustingly tied the piece of red thread around my wrist. But with long sleeves it became even more difficult to find the right wrist. I nearly always managed to reduce the class to chaos, the teacher to screams and the clapper to a quicker and quicker tempo. Eventually, teacher decided that with me in the class, physical exercises would be safer if they consisted of floor exercises, ball games and other activities, where it was not necessary to make a decision as to where was right and where was left. Somehow, I must have started very early to be different. It was no joy, I wanted to be just like everybody else.

Eventually, I did learn to write with my right hand but practised writing with my left at home and developed a useful parlour trick in writing with both hands at the same time. When, some years later I fell and broke my right wrist, my ability to write with my left hand, although frowned upon in school, nevertheless came in useful.

DANCING WAS SOMETHING I really loved to do, passionately. From the time I was about four I went, together with lots of other little girls, to dancing class. It was supposed to be ballet but we were told that we were not allowed to do point work until aged twelve because it would ruin our feet, so we had only soft ballet slippers. In any case, teacher really preferred us to be barefoot because that way she could tell that we were pointing our toes in the approved way. The classes were one of a number held in a basement hall. Quite big girls were before us and even grown-ups went there to do proper ballet. I was a tubby child with mousy hair, the natural wave of which was kept strictly controlled under a slide because that was the fashion, unless you were blond and curly like Shirley Temple. Nor was I of a particularly sylph-like shape, I did not have much of a waist and was really a bit dumpy. But none of that stopped me from thinking and believing that I was very graceful. I never got fed up, like some other little girls, of doing *pliés* in the five positions and all the rest of the bar work. After all, I could kick my legs as high as anyone, even allowing for the fact that I was not very tall and, eventually, could achieve all the acrobatic feats required to reach a very satisfactory standard, except for never being able to do the splits really well.

I had been going to dancing classes for over three years

when the new exhibition building was completed in Bratislava and the President was to come to the official opening. That was going to be something really exciting. The ceremony was to be held in the main Exhibition Hall and, knowing that Thomas Masaryk liked children very much, all the children's organisations were asked to co-operate in laying on a performance. My dancing school was very fortunate in the draw and a specially choreographed dance at the close of the proceedings was to be performed by the children of eight years or under. It was decided that it should be based on Slovak folk dances, that we should be dressed in the three national colours red, white and blue, represented by the appropriate flowers; poppies, daisies and cornflowers and that the final tableaux should represent the national flag. Organising three dozen little girls of that age is not easy. It was decided that there were going to be three groups of twelve and that each group should be led by the smallest child. Was I glad that I was small! I did dance quite well and now I was going to come into my own, bliss. I was going to lead the poppies.

I don't know who was more excited, Mother or me. The costumes were being made by a dressmaker and I can still remember every detail. There was a shiny satin top with shoelace straps, the *dernier cri* of fashion at the time. Below it, a very full net tutu in red or blue or white depending on which flower you were, with large silk flowers scattered over the skirt and a big flower on the left shoulder. Ballet slippers of the appropriate colour accompanied along with a wreath of poppies, daisies or cornflowers with trailing ribbons down the back and, for the leader, a silver wand with red, white or blue streamers. It seemed to me that there were simply weeks and weeks of rehearsals and preparations. On the floor of our dance hall the size of the stage was marked out in white chalk and the shape of the flag was also marked out to ensure that we would be in the right position at the end of the dance.

We did not practise in our costumes but in our normal ballet wear. The marvellous, shimmering outfit hung outside the wardrobe, sheathed with a white cover to prevent it getting dusty. Every so often, probably very often, I peeked under it in wonder and anyone who came to our home had to be shown it in all its glory, and be told that not only was I going to dance in front of the President and hundreds of other people but, also, that I had been singled out to lead them.

The day before the big one there was a dress rehearsal at the exhibition hall. Backstage, with all the scaffolding, it did not look half as glamorous as at the front of the house and there were hundreds of children milling around, orders being shouted out, bits of music played; a general confusion. I, an eight-year-old introverted child, found this all rather frightening and disturbing. Mother was with me and we tried to keep close to my dancing teacher but so were another thirty-five children with their mothers. Dora, our teacher, clapped her hands, 'Daisies on the left, poppies on the right, cornflowers in the middle. Are you ready? Remember, when the music starts the daisies come first, then the poppies and finally the cornflowers. Stop jostling each other! The leaders in front, have you got your wands? And line up in pairs behind the leader. Quiet there! When the music starts, look at me and come out at my signal, as we have rehearsed it. Ready?'

The music started. Blonde Olga led out the daisies, they hopped in a circle around the stage, formed a line, hopped some more, formed a double line and after more hopping came to rest on the left side of the stage in three lines, the first one crouching down, the second one behind them on one knee and the third one standing up; a more or less solid block of white daisies. Before the last line had settled, it was time for the poppies to come out, led by me, perform more or less the same manoeuvres, coming to rest on the right side of the stage. No mishap so far. Finally, the cornflowers took centre stage and, after the obligatory hopping, formed a triangular shape between the daisies and the poppies and the tableau of the national flag was complete. Dora was satisfied, it looked good and was most appropriate. After a few words of encouragement and the odd admonition, we were allowed to go home to prepare for the huge occasion.

To say that I was nervous was an understatement. I could not hold still, had to keep on looking at the poppy dress, try out the wand, swinging it from side to side as if directing armies of poppies to the right, to the left and in any other possible direction. Eventually Mother managed to get me to bed, I thought I'd be too excited to sleep but did nonetheless.

Next morning there was no chance of me having any breakfast, by now my inability to hold down food in the morning was well known. Father suggested a little nip of something stronger, to give me Dutch courage but Mother vetoed that, I could not go and meet others reeking of strong drink. Having managed about two bites of bread, Mother and I and the costume took the tram to the Exhibition Hall. Father and the rest of the family, who naturally had tickets to see the performance, would come on later.

Things were very busy backstage. There were lots of other performers but that did not interest us. After all, we were to go on last, to be the apotheosis of the whole performance.

Mothers and helpers were allowed to get us into our costumes and then had to leave. We sat down in lines, each set of flowers separately so as not to get mixed up. And then something awful happened to me. All the excitement was affecting my innards and it seemed to me that a storm was brewing in my tummy.

I shouted out, 'Please Miss Dora, I've got to go!'

'Go where?' She said surprised.

I was wracked in confusion, how could I convey politely my extreme need?

'I need the toilet,' was all I could manage.

'You should have gone before you put your costume on.'

'I did. But now I need to go! Now, very much!' I began shouting.

Miss Dora sighed with exasperation. 'All right, Mary will take you.' Mary was Miss Dora's helper. Anyone else?'

Nobody was afflicted as I was. The toilets were outside in a tent, a line of cubicles with canvas doors and inside each cubicle a wooden box with a lid and a bucket underneath. Some cut-up newspapers on a piece of string. Not in my wildest dreams would I have entered such a place under normal circumstances. I would have tied myself in knots rather than go into that horrible smelly area but I had no choice. I drew my breath, held it, entered quickly, pulled down my knickers, sat down and submitted to the worst attack of diarrhoea imaginable.

Outside, Mary called, 'Are you done yet? Hurry up!'

She could just as well have asked me to be a fairy on top of a Christmas tree.

'I haven't finished – I'll never finish,' I wailed.

'Oh, dear,' said Mary, 'you better hurry. There are only ten minutes before you go on. I've got to go and see that everybody is ready. I'll tell Miss Dora.'

I burst into tears, which precipitated another surge. There was no way I could leave this horrible place. The smell, by now I was the smell, it was so horrible. I don't know how long I stayed there but it must have been some time. I heard the music that introduced our piece but I was not there to lead the poppies, I was tethered to this horrible place by my guts that tried to turn me inside out. I cried and cried.

Meanwhile, outside in the auditorium, Mother and Father, Grandma and Grandpa sat up straight when the daisies came on, to better see me leading the poppies. The poppies came on but no Iby. What had happened? Mother immediately rushed from her seat, came backstage and demanded to know where I was. She started to call my name. Miss Dora shushed her and explained to her that I had become suddenly unwell.

'Where is she? Have you called a doctor? An ambulance?' she said, clearly worried.

Miss Dora explained that I was in the toilet.

'Who is with the poor child?' Mother asked.

'I think Mary is with her.'

'Oh, no, Miss Dora, I am here,' she said. 'I had to come and help you.'

'And you left that poor child all on her own? Eight years old? How could you?'

The next thing I heard was Mother's voice, calling my name. 'I'm here!' I cried.

I was so relieved to hear Mother that I felt I could, nearly, get off the bucket except that I couldn't because I had used up all the cut-up newspapers. But Mother was here, all would be well. I got cleaned up and we all went home, me feeling rather weak.

My disappointment at not having been able to dance in front of the President was enormous and the feeling that I had let down Miss Dora stayed with me for a long time.

Another aspect that stayed with me to this day is that my insides get into turmoil when I am stressed.

GENERALLY, WE CHILDREN HAD to be in bed comparatively early, after all we had to be in school by eight in the morning. That meant getting up no later than half past six. I never liked getting up and early mornings were, and still are, anathema to me. By the time we arose, the *Kacheloffen*, the tall tiled stove in the living room was warm as the fire was banked up late at night. Breakfast time, in particular, was a nightmare for me until I was about ten. Normally for the youngsters, it consisted of a bowl of hot, sweetened milk with a teaspoon of coffee in it - a concession - into which we dunked fresh crispy rolls. The milk and rolls were gathered each morning by the younger of our two servants, the elder one was always the cook. The milk was collected from a little corner shop in a white enamel jug with a domed lid which fitted inside and was on a short chain so that it could never fall off and get dirty. The rolls were put in a basket lined with a white cloth. They were hot and freshly baked, except on weekends, when there was instead homemade brioche. They were considered too rich for young stomachs, we had just plain bread and butter at weekends. Bread was always made at home but baked at the bakery two streets away. The bakery was in a basement and one could look through the window at pavement level at the half-stripped bakers at work at the ovens, using long- handled shovels to put the dough in and bring the bread out. The younger maid took the dough to the bakery in an oblong, narrow wicker basket wrapped in a white cloth and she wore a snow white apron and cap. The basket and cloth were left at the baker with the dough so that the bread could be brought back in the same receptacle. What I could never understand, as a child, was how an oblong piece of dough got transformed into a large flattish round, crunchy crusted loaf of bread which had to sit on top of the basket, like a fat toad. The bread smelled and tasted sweet and sour, of dough and crust and sometimes of caraway seeds. It lasted us a week. How awful it was when the heel of last week's had to be finished off although the new bread had arrived and was filling the apartment with its lovely smell.

The Woman Without A Number

The privilege of cutting the first slice, to spread it thickly with butter and to eat it, nodding approval, belonged to Father. Nobody touched the bread before him. I remember, when I was in my early teens, resenting that Father had that first one, that coveted corner and we just got slices especially as I liked the crusts better than the inside of the bread. Once, I cut a slice with a corner off aslant – and then realizing that the loaf looked somewhat odd, did the same on the other side. Naturally, they were not even; I never mastered the art of cutting bread straight. So a bit more got cut off from the first side, then some more from the other side and a bit more here and there and in the end the loaf looked as if rather large mice had nibbled it and those crusts were divine. When cook discovered what I had done she was not amused, nor was my brother's Nanny nor my Governess, nor Mother, but somehow Father, as usual, saw the funny side of it.

The reason that breakfast was such a problem for me was due to milk. I didn't like it and it, apparently, did not like me either. Morning after morning, before going to school, breakfast and I parted company. But milk was good for you, a child had to have it and that it did not remain with me long enough to do me any good was due, after consultation with Dr Meyer, our doctor and family friend, to my nervous stomach. After that, I was allowed to go to school without having more than one sip of milky coffee and I had to take two thin slices of buttered bread wrapped in greaseproof paper and a napkin with me to school. This I had to eat in the first break and my Governess came to the railings of the playground and collected the napkin and took it home as proof that I had. In about the third year of the primary school, milk was introduced. Skimmed milk or a milky chocolate drink in a bottle was available to any of us, if we wanted it. These icy cold drinks were welcome, especially in the summer and chocolate, even in milk, was different. We all drank it, including me. The chocolate milk drink never disagreed with me and neither my parents nor anyone at home knew that I could drink chocolate milk even with my nervous stomach. It took fifty years to find out that I had an allergy to the fats in milk and for many years as an adult I went without breakfast, thinking it was breakfast that inconvenienced my stomach, rather than that.

FATHER'S FAMILY APPEARED TO be spread around the world. Two sisters, Aunt Teresa and Aunt Bella lived in Budapest but his brother emigrated just after World War One to the USA. Two of Father's cousins, Aunt Aurelia and Aunt Elsie, had been opera singers at the Komische Opera in Berlin. Aunt Aurelia, the one with corn-gold hair was seen performing by an English Lord who fell in love with her, married her and whisked her off to England. Aurelia would not be separated from her sister, so Elsie went too. They had a town house in Greenwich which was requisitioned in the Second World War by the Admiralty, while she, her son Aurel and Elsie, spent the war years in the States. By this time she was either widowed or divorced, whichever, since no husband was in evidence. Before the War, Aurel and I were introduced to each other. I was probably about ten and he, a few years older, a typically thin, lanky, spotty teenager. We did not take to each other but that did not worry our respective mothers who planned that we should marry in due course. They were confident that things would be different between us when we were older and more sensible. Fat chance!

Some years before this encounter it was decided that it was quite imperative that I should become proficient in English. The British Consulate was only three doors away from our apartment. Among the staff were native English speakers and Mother's aim was that I should learn English from one of them and that no accent should taint my speech. I already spoke Hungarian to Father, who never managed to learn another language, Slovakian to the maids, German in school and Hungarian, Slovak or German to Mother. I found it very difficult to decide which was really my native tongue.

Mother called at the consulate and explained that she was looking for an English teacher for her daughter. Although most of the staff was male, there was a secretary who had a sister living with her and she was likely to be willing to give me English lessons. An appointment was made for me and mother to meet the Misses. I have forgotten their names, if I ever knew them, because I only addressed them as 'Miss'. They lived in a little house, like a gingerbread cottage, built in a quasi-Tudor style which was crammed with furniture, knick-knacks, antimacassars and lace doilies, all sorts of things which did not exist in our home. The house was in the grounds of the consulate.

It was usual for people to have their names on a brass plate on or near their front door. In the case of the two Misses, there was an elaborate brass letterbox, engraved with the word 'LETTERS' and I naturally assumed that this was their name. So for me they were always the Misses Letters.

I don't think that Miss Letters was a particularly good teacher although she did try to educate me, not only in the English language but also manners and etiquette, on which she was very hot. After a time, Mother was quite perturbed about the mincing way in which I would lift my cup, extending my little finger ever so carefully, nibbling at little pieces of cake, crossing my ankles, never my knees, and speaking softly. This phase did not last very long though, my natural spirit could not conform to the straightjacket of near-Victorian ways. I went twice a week to Miss Letters, getting a good grounding in English grammar, in the difference between should, would and could as well as shall and will. Miss Letters told me that it was easy and so it was after the tortuous grammar of the German language, which was being drilled into me at school. When I was about ten, the lessons ceased and I think that the Misses Letters went back to England, into retirement. By that time I did speak English quite well but with a limited vocabulary and English literature was a closed book to me. It was to be remedied by my next English teacher, the flautist with the Bratislava Symphony orchestra.

Music was always an important part of my life. Sunday night at home was 'music night'. Father played the violin, another violinist and a viola player joined him and on occasions when the many stairs to our apartment did not daunt him too much and he had not had too much wine with his dinner, there was even a cello player.

Aunt Janka lived in the mezzanine with her solicitor and landowner husband, Uncle George, who spent his days reading the papers and waiting for clients to turn up. His numerous family members frequently came to visit to get some city air and to bring his share of the produce as payment in kind. Although vegetables and fruit came more or less regularly from the estate, it was not enough to live on and Aunt Janka had to take in lodgers to make ends meet. It was not generally known as it would have been considered a disgrace that she, who had married a rich landowner, now had to act as servant to others. There was a spare room overlooking the garden that was let to a flautist with the Bratislava Symphony Orchestra, who also claimed to be a poet and who taught English. There was a large conservatory, which was let out to a different gentleman. It was much desired because it had a separate entrance from the garden, however, it was only habitable during the summer months as there were no means of heating it. A section of the large hallway had also been partitioned off and this lead to a small room and a washroom. This mini apartment was let to a quiet, mousy lady. Uncle George did not, in principle, approve of lady lodgers, but could not find fault with Miss Mousy. The flat also had its own garden, rather than having to share the large one with the other residents. It became a useful adjunct to the household; vegetables and salad stuffs were grown there, even melons and sunflowers for their seeds. A couple of trees provided shade and fruit. Uncle George didn't garden but we children liked to help Aunt Janka, because we only had a walnut and a pear tree and a large swing in our part. I tried growing scarlet runner beans once, against the wire fence at the back, because they looked so pretty. They lost the battle against the bindweed and never produced any beans but then bindweed also had pretty flowers.

The gentlemen lodgers were provided with breakfast, which they could either consume in the kitchen or in their own rooms and there was, evidently, no objection to them bringing back the odd cold cut for their dinner. After all, breakfast was only coffee, bread, butter and jam. The front room facing the street was Uncle George's office; the ornately furnished sitting and dining rooms and the elaborate pear-wood bedroom furniture presented an image of opulence. The kitchen was dire, Aunt Janka didn't have a servant, so she had to do everything herself. Housekeeping in those days was hard work and Aunt Janka's beauty began to fade prematurely. They had one daughter, Magda, the same age as my brother, and she spend much of the time with us.

The flautist soon became a permanent member of Father's music group, even popping up sometimes during the week to play a duet with him and he encouraged me to accompany. He often gave us tickets to concerts. Mother tolerated the music but did not participate. The flautist was always welcomed to stay for a meal, the servants thought that he had a very good nose for he could always smell when there was something especially nice and would appear about an hour before dinnertime. With the Misses Letters gone, Mother felt that I should continue my studies at the appropriate level and also learn about English literature. So when she found out that the flautist spoke fluent English, she saw her opportunity and arrangements were made for me to continue my English lessons with him. It was not considered appropriate, of course, that I should visit him in his room, so he came upstairs to us on two afternoons to teach me and then stay for dinner, unless he had a musical engagement. Financial terms acceptable to both parties were agreed.

I must have been not much older than 12 and I had developed a bust early. I was only too aware of it, although there were no other indications of sexual maturity. Talk about sex among us girls at High School became more and more interesting especially when one of the girls came back from the summer holiday and gave us a reasonably graphic description of the tumble in the hay she had experienced while staying on her grandparents' farm. Whether it was fact or fiction we could not determine, after all the rest of us were still entirely innocent, most of us had not even been kissed by a boy. She certainly rose in our esteem and whether she had gone 'all the way' or not remained a topic of conversation for a long time.

I tried to find something out about the facts of life. Obviously I could not ask Father and Mother said I was far too young, so that left only Fraulein Trude, my brother's German nanny. I was having a bath. The bath itself had a wooden cover

257

that could be removed and which extended more than halfway over it. It had originally been made to hold the baby bath for my brother but it proved useful later on, too. For one thing, it was possible for a person to be immersed in the bath and someone else could come in, stoke the fire or wash their hands without privacy being too much disturbed. Later on the big copper boiler was removed and instead a geyser was installed, for which I had a healthy respect because of the noise it made, like an explosion, when it was turned on.

I was luxuriating in the hot water, watching my fingers become prune-like and trying to see whether I could put my big toe into the tap while Fraulein Trude was washing something in the basin. This was my opportunity to acquire knowledge. By this time I was pretty certain that gestation for a human was nine months but something else was puzzling me.

'Fraulein is it true that it takes nine months for a baby to grow in its mother's tummy before it is born,' I asked.

'Yes,' replied Fraulein.

'Well,' I said, 'How is it that Johanna (an acquaintance of ours) had a baby in only seven months after she was married?'

'It is possible for babies to be born early,' she replied. 'They come when they are ready and some of them are ready after seven months. They are usually smaller, though, than babies which had had nine months to develop.'

'But Joanna's baby weighed more than five kilos: I heard her mother say that they thought she would have twins.'

'Such things happen,' replied Fraulein Trude.

'But then,' I carried on, 'why did Katarina's baby die? She had been pregnant for eight months. Why is seven months all right but eight months not?'

'I have no idea,' said Fraulein, who usually set herself up as the oracle on anything to do with the body, but did not

258

want to mar my innocence by explaining all the fuss that had preceded Johanna's shotgun marriage. I was no wiser.

By this time we had Natural Science at school. It was a mixture of rather basic biology and botany. Our teacher, who had been a medical doctor, refused to use the textbook but drew lurid diagrams on the blackboard, expecting us to take notes at extreme speed and was especially keen to talk to us about human biology. The explanation of human reproduction was, however, so dense and mysterious that I never understood any of it. I often wondered why he was replaced with a student teacher after only two months. We ran rings around this new teacher, who used a boring textbook which did not mention humans and who blushed even when talking about birds laying eggs.

My English, though, was progressing. Having swam with ease through the textbook *Englisch lernen ein Vergnugen,* (Learning English is fun) my new teacher thought that to combine language with literature was best done by reading, translating and explaining the plays of Oscar Wilde. I remember *The Importance of Being Earnest*, and *Lady Windermere's Fan*. The explanations of the *double entendre* certainly enlarged my knowledge and learning was certainly fun.

We were having lessons upstairs, in my room, which had a large pink *Kacheloffen* in the corner. Leaning against it on cold days and letting the warmth seep through to your bones was lovely. My teacher musician also wrote German poetry. I now know that it was pornographic but did not at that time, all I understood was that it rhymed. One or two of his collections had been published and he gave them to me to read, advising me not to tell my parents about it. I was innocent enough not to query why, nor did I really understand what they were about. He probably thought that I did because some of the versification had a lovely sound to it and I had memorised them. Leaning against the *Kacheloffen* I recited one I had remembered, having no idea what it was all about. The next thing I knew, I had been thrown onto my bed, which was a settee in the daytime, and I was raped. Only I did not know what was being done to me. I just knew I did not want to have any more English lessons and told my mother so.

14

*

The Start Of The Nightmare

By the mid-1930s, the newspapers had plenty to write about events in Germany, but like any other just-teenage girl, international news was not of prime importance to me. What was much more interesting was whether I would be able to get away with going to the pictures while pretending to be over sixteen, so that I could see *Tarzan* and *Ben Hur*. The make-up on mother's dressing table was raided and it must have worked, because I can still remember the thrill of seeing those films.

I first became aware that events in Germany were going to affect me when mother told me one summer day at the end of my third year in the German High School that I would not be going there the next year. Since I loved the High School and had a crush on my form teacher, Karl Hausknecht, I threw a tantrum and asked mother what I had done that was so wrong that she was taking me away from school and all my friends. She consoled me that I had done nothing wrong but that she had been to see Mr Hausknecht at school and had explained to him that she wanted to

261

prevent my being excluded. Mr Hausknecht had been most complimentary about my use of the German language. He told her that I was top in composition and poetry and was most upset that mother was taking me away because, although he was a member of the German National Socialist Party, he could not envisage that I would ever be excluded. By this time, a few of my stories and poems had been published in the local papers and also in an anthology of students' work. Mother's reply had been that if I were indeed a talented writer in the making then I would succeed regardless of the language in which lessons were at a school. In retrospect, I do not think that she was right; I never managed to write in Czech, Slovak or Hungarian with the wealth of language I had used in German and it took many years of living in England before I felt able to let my writing take wings.

Arrangements were made for me to start the next academic year at the 1st Masaryk High School, one with a high academic reputation where the teaching languages were Slovak and Czech and, because there were very few girls in the school, I gradually came to the conclusion that it might not be a bad changeover. There was one disadvantage, I had to spend the summer holidays with a tutor learning Slovak and Czech grammar and also re-learning science subjects like physics, chemistry and natural sciences in Czech, which I found exceedingly difficult. When the academic year started, the walk to the Masaryk High School was considerably longer than to my previous one. There were only seventeen girls in the whole school with 800 boys and our class size was also much smaller than it had been at the German High School.

Mother, though, had been correct in her assumptions. The following year, Jewish students were excluded from the German High School. What neither she nor anyone else had anticipated was that after the Germans had occupied Bohemia and Tiso, a Catholic Priest would became head of the Government in Slovakia and decreed boys and girls were not allowed to be educated in the same school, so another change ensured.

We girls had to leave the 1st Masaryk High School and, since Mother didn't think a Catholic school was quite right for me, I went to a Protestant Girls' school at the other end of town. The redeeming feature was that across the street was a boys school and we could communicate by holding up written messages from window to window until we were severely reprimanded. I found the ethos of the girls' school, where most of the teachers were female and members of the religious order, very peculiar.

One of my best friends was my cousin Gertie. Whereas I went to the High School, she had gone to the Secondary School and, after the fourth year, to the College of Commerce to learn shorthand, typing, bookkeeping and other commercial subjects. After I left the German High School we were thrown together quite a lot because I was too proud to look up my German friends and did not make friends with anyone in the other schools. Gertie was brought up quite strictly. Edith, her older sister, was allowed to go dancing, chaperoned by my mother, who herself adored dancing. Gertie and I spent time together, mainly in the garden discussing the fortunes of members of the family. We did not seem to have much else in common. That she also finished up in England and that, for a time, our lives became again intertwined, belongs to another story.

The first thing that the Slovak Government did was to nationalise all Jewish businesses. This was done by putting in 'a reliable person' to supervise the running of the business and to cream off the profits. The person nominated to come into our shop was a one legged, very odd man who sat on a chair in front of the main counter so as not to miss anything that was going on. However, not very far from us, there was a pub and with the extra money he spent long lunch times there. Mother realised that by providing a supply of liquor also at the shop he was all but asleep in his chair if he wasn't in the pub. As far as the running of the business was concerned, as long as he had enough money for drink he wasn't worried. Nominally, he was now the owner but he had about as much knowledge of engineering as the office cat.

It was some distance to the school and I had to take a bus and a tram for the journey. The next rule that came out was forbidding the use of public transport to people who were Jewish. This caused a lot of problems because it was not always obvious who was. Shops were not opened because people could not get to them, staff didn't turn up and chaos reigned. The Government's solution was simple; identify people who are Jewish, let them use the public transport but don't let them sit down. To do that, yellow badges in the shape of the Star of David were issued to all Jews and the order went out that they had to be worn at all times, even on their nightwear, the reasoning being that if there was a fire at night, people wearing a yellow star would have a lesser chance of being rescued.

I had a battle with my parents about this yellow star because I did not want to wear it. I had many friends who did not know I was Jewish and I felt certain that I would embarrass them if I wore the star. It would also make it impossible for me to join them on trips to cafés, walks or anywhere else. I didn't feel I could put them to the test; there were only two options, to wear the star and no longer see my friends or not to wear the star and be liable to instant imprisonment.

The journey to school became particularly fraught. Unless the weather was particularly bad I preferred to get up earlier and walk there with a scarf hiding the tell-tale star rather than exposing it on public transport and having frequent harassment. If I did go on the bus I ensured that I was right at the back of it, turned with my back to the front of it. In school, the teachers had decreed that, whereas the yellow star had to be worn on outer clothes, as far as they were concerned they refused to allow it to be worn in class. By this time there were only two of us in the class to whom it applied. The whole situation made me tremendously angry. I felt I wanted to hit out and retaliate in some sort of way but did not know how. I heard of a Jewish youth group called *Betar* and decided to join them. They were mainly boys but the odd thing was that gradually groups of boys disappeared. After persistent questioning I was told that they were being smuggled to Palestine to work in the underground group *Irgun zvai Leumi* and that they would be instrumental in establishing a Zionist state in Palestine. Girls were not wanted; in any case, by no stretch of imagination would my parents have let me go.

SUMMER HOLIDAYS FROM SCHOOL were long and Mother considered it important that they should be usefully occupied. When I was twelve, I spent most of them with Granny, who taught me to cook and bake, a skill in which Mother was deficient. Granny also showed me to knit and crochet because I had been unable to learn that in school due to my preference for the left hand and the teacher's inability to address it. When I was fourteen, I spent the summer holiday with a dressmaker where I was taught to take measurements properly, to make a paper pattern and to sew. Whereas every other youngster being tutored brought some plain fabric to make a simple blouse I had to be different and turned up with pure silk containing a pattern of tiny flowers and a desire to make a blouse with small pin tucks instead of a dart. It took me longer to make but it became one of my favourite garments and taught me much more than making a simple blouse would have done. Next we were to make a skirt. Naturally, I did not choose to make a plain up and down one, but one with pleats all round. Again, many useful techniques were discovered. My final effort of a bias-cut dress with a collar of Brussels lace taxed mine and the dressmaker's patience, but I made it and it certainly did not look homemade. I wore this dress, without its lace colour, just plain black, to have a professional photo taken when I was fifteen.

Being able to sew had its disadvantages too, it meant that I was now considered able to darn and mend. So as not to be bored by repairing the large holes that were inevitable in the wool and cotton socks worn, I devised all sorts of fancy stitches which made the darn prettier and often stronger than normal, however, it did not make the socks very comfortable to wear.

I did like to do embroidery, though, especially petit point, and proceeded to make new covers for the Rococo drawing room chairs. Each chair took the best part of a year to do but these new tapestry covers were practically indestructible and better than the threadbare original gold brocade. They survived the war years and Mother got them back. The chairs finished up in a museum in Bratislava.

THINGS GOT WORSE. OUR apartment, in the best part of the town, was requisitioned for German officers. We had to leave and we were given a small flat on the Mileticova Street. It consisted of two rooms, a kitchen and a bathroom. Some people had much worse places. Before we left Palisady, Mother buried hers and Aunt Janka's silver plate under the bottom step of Aunt Janka's conservatory. I can't remember where Aunt Janka and her family went when they too were forced out. Mother's biggest problem was what to do with all our furniture. There was no way it could fit into the flat. She arranged for the drawing room furniture to be taken into the country to Topolcianky, from where all our servant girls had come for generations. The other stuff was somehow wedged into the two rooms. But where would Tomy and I sleep? A board was constructed to fit over the bath and Tomy's mattress was put on top at night. The kitchen was just like a corridor and I had a narrow folding bed there. Once the bed was put up I had to get into it from the bottom, it just fitted between the sink and the cooker and nothing in the kitchen was then accessible. We were fortunate that the previous owners of the flat had had a telephone and Mother managed to get it connected which was quite a lifeline as it turned out.

Most of our friends and relatives who lived in a fashionable area had their apartments or houses requisitioned. My grandparents had to leave their small retirement flat and were put into a tiny primitive cottage in a small village just outside Bratislava. Since there were just the two of them, they were only allowed a single room with a kitchen and an outside lavatory. By this time grandfather was suffering severely from dropsy and life for grandmother must have been extremely difficult. I seemed to spend most of my time in queues for food. Being served in a shop was an obstacle race. Shopkeepers had been instructed that as long as one non-Jewish person was in the shop they had to be served before any Jewish ones, so even to get a single loaf of bread could take hours. Since we were only shopping for food and other essentials and we tended to frequent the shops we had used previously, the situation was quite embarrassing for the shopkeepers.

The Woman Without A Number

After we moved to the Mileticova Street, a long distance from our previous home, we had to use shops where we were not known and could not expect any preferential treatment. By now, any Jewish food shops had Aryan overseers and owners so the same restrictions applied there too. It was not unknown for the new owner's friends to come and buy up the scarce resources. By the time my turn came there was frequently no bread and certainly no meat at the butchers.

My parents still went to the shop that had been 'nationalised' but now as employees of the one-legged peasant owner. As I was not allowed to continue my education in the High School on account of the Jewish Law, which restricted education for Jews, I was told to refrain from my 'intellectual pretensions.' I enrolled in a class to learn graphic design despite being told by my teacher when I was nine years old that I could not draw. I had taken endless trouble at home to produce a circular design for a tile in two colour-ways and teacher just would not believe that it was my own, unaided work. Neither of my parents would have dreamt of helping me with homework and the nanny's duties did not extend to that either.

I really enjoyed the course, designing posters for concerts, talks and meetings, learning about proportions, affinity and contrast of colours. We also did some bookbinding, designing and hand-painting end papers and similar tasks. I was especially proud of my work on a presentation copy of a collection of Slovak folksongs, which I bound in hand woven heavy linen on the cover of which I had painted an abstract interpretation of a traditional folk design. The course lasted just six months as our teacher decided to emigrate illegally to Israel.

At least not being allowed to go to school had the advantage of not going out and having to wear that hated yellow star. I thought it was an extreme example of stigmatisation. I did not feel different from anyone else, so why was I being marked in this way? It instilled in me a deep shame about being Jewish. We lived cooped up in our tiny flat. Father used to go out to meet his cronies and to play chess in the one remaining Jewish coffee house; Mother would visit and help Grandmother whenever she could, which meant an hour's journey each way. I was busy with Nick, my boyfriend, using snatched moments in unlikely places to make love. Time was precious, we did not know what the future would hold, so the present had to be enjoyed. Nick was one of those who did not come back.

One evening, in the early spring of 1942, we had been at home in that cramped, over-furnished flat when Hugo, Mother's cousin, who refused to wear a yellow star, visited us. It was past the curfew hour but as Hugo did not wear a star and had, as I knew, false ID papers, he disregarded it. The phone rang. It was the distraught voice of the mother of one of my friends. She told mother that 'they' had been and taken her daughter. She asked whether they had also taken me, whether she knew where they were taking the girls. By this time more and more of my new-found friends had quietly disappeared, left the country or gone into hiding. Edith and Gertie, my cousins and their two brothers, Karl and Béla had left, illegally, for Israel some time ago. The boys had arrived but the boat on which the girls were had been stopped at sea and they had been interned in Italy. Eventually they reached Israel. Mother, thinking quickly, said that I was not staying at home at present, a euphemism we all used to indicate that someone had gone.

No time could now be lost, 'they' could be on their way to the flat. Into a small old suitcase went a change of clothing, I put on an old coat and covered my head with a kerchief in the way that Slovak peasant girls did. Hugo was going to take me to my grandparents until Mother could organise something more permanent for me. Whether Mother ever blamed my father for the fact that I had not left earlier I never knew. I could have gone long before, there had been so many plans and half-hearted arrangements, not least the Kindertransport to Britain but they came to nothing because he could not bear to be parted from me, his *'Liebling'*.

On a rattling old tram, pretending to be kissing and cuddling, Hugo and I travelled to the end of the line and then started to walk to my grandparent's cottage. Hugo woke grandmother. He explained to her that I had to be hidden but that it would not be for long and that nobody was to know I was there. If anyone asked, they should say that I had left without asking permission from my parents and nobody knew where I had gone. Hugo explained that he could not stay as he had to be back at work in the morning. Whether he managed to get a tram back or walked all the way I never found out. I slept that night and the next on a mattress on the kitchen floor. I had to be quiet and hid under grandfather's bed if anyone came to the cottage.

Mother must have been hectically busy trying to arrange some way of smuggling me out of the country. The third evening, on Saturday, Hugo came back, this time wheeling two bicycles. Most unlike him, he was not in his usual smart clothes but in old trousers, tucked into his socks, an old jacket, a cap and muffler. This time he stayed the night, also sleeping on the kitchen floor. The bicycles were the plain black, utility models, Army issue ones, no chromium bits, nothing shining on them. Early next evening, we set off ostensibly going to visit friends in the next village, both of us looking like peasants out for an evening call. Hugo had also brought a bundle with some more clothes for me and also some money, both Slovak and Hungarian currency.

I was not familiar with the countryside through which we rode. After cycling for more than an hour, we stopped in a lane with fields on one side and a wood on the other. Out of the wood stepped a man I did not know, also wheeling a bicycle. He and Hugo went some distance from me, Hugo handed him something and they came back. Hugo gave me a quick hug and said, 'Good luck, girl.' He got on his bike and went back the way we had come.

The man got on his bicycle, motioned to me to do the same and we set off. It was not far. We came to a small village, got off the bikes and the man motioned me to be quiet. We wheeled them along the deserted lane. By the side of a cottage we leant them against the wall. He tapped the door gently and it was opened by a friendly, buxom woman, Mariska, who waved us in. She also motioned us to be quiet. We were in a big kitchen and two children were asleep in the wall bed. We took off our shoes, tiptoed out of the kitchen into the small parlour, with its stiff furniture.

'Tired?' she asked. I nodded.

'Hungry?' I shook my head.

'Thirsty?' I nodded.

She went out and came back with a glass of milk, the one item of food I could not bear but on this occasion I drank it, hoping that it would stay in my stomach, because, as she showed me later, all the 'facilities' were out of doors, at the bottom of the garden. It was usual for the curtains to be drawn in the parlour. A makeshift bed had been made up for me on the sofa. She told me to get some sleep, to put a chair under the door handle to prevent a child accidentally coming in and under no circumstances to make any noise until she came for me. She would give three knocks three times. The next morning I heard her getting the two little girls ready for school. I listened to their chatter and laughter. After they had left she knocked, as arranged. By this time I was anxious to visit the 'facilities.' Mariska made certain that there was nobody about and came with me, waiting outside, to make certain that the coast was also clear for me to return to the house. Bread, butter and coffee were produced and we sat down to concoct a story that would account for my presence. Hugo had told me that Mother thought that it would take a few days for my onward journey to be arranged. Mariska and I discussed who I could be and eventually we decided that I would be her niece who had come to spend a few days with them because my mother, her sister, had to go into hospital. Since her niece had not visited before, we thought that the story would hold water. It was generally known that her sister was in poor health, a widow who lived on the outskirts of Bratislava.

I wondered how to occupy my time. Except for the family Bible, there were no books. The cottage consisted of the large kitchen with the wall-bed, a small bedroom and that neat, stuffy parlour where I had slept and which was used only for visits by the priest and for the laying out of a corpse. Housework was minimal, except for cooking and baking, in which Mariska was much more proficient than I. But there was one skill I had, the use of the needle.

I asked Mariska whether she had any sewing to be done.

She looked doubtful.

'Mending?' she asked.

'Yes.' I said, 'but I can also make new clothes.'

'We only have new clothes for the children at Easter and I haven't bought any stuff for that yet. But there is some darning. Can you do that?'

Darning was not exactly my favourite pastime, but I had learned to do a lot of fancy darning stitches.

'Of course,' I said.

'How fortunate,' said Mariska. 'I never have a chance to get to the bottom of the darning basket.'

That was not really surprising. The darning basket with which I was presented was a half-barrel and it was overflowing with socks, most of them not paired.

'Do you mind if I sort them first?' I asked.

'Do whatever you like with them, as long as some of them can be used again. My mother says she cannot keep up with knitting socks, we seem to get through so many.'

So I set about sorting, first by colour, then by size and then, hopefully, by size of hole. I finished up with a pile of socks with holes of manageable size and another larger one with holes through which I could push my fist. I re-filled the barrel, putting the worst socks on the bottom and set to. I thought that in that way I would show some quick results. By the end of the first day, I had repaired and paired several pairs of socks and Mariska admired my tidy darning. In the next two days the bigger holes were darned with fancy stitches, not only because that was more interesting for me but also because it produced a firmer texture and was less likely to become a hole again in a hurry. By the end of the second day, when there were not many more socks in the barrel Mariska asked, 'John has some shirts where the collar has frayed, could you darn those?'

'I can do better than that,' I replied. 'Have you a sewing machine?'

'Of course, it came from your shop,' said Mariska proudly.

'In that case I can turn the collars and the cuffs and the shirts will be as good as new. Mind you the cuffs will be a little narrower.'

So, three shirts had their collars and cuffs turned, a job that required a lot of patience in unpicking the existing stitches. Two of the girls' dresses had to have the hem let down so that they could last another year. I never got to the bottom of the darning barrel, though. On the fourth day, after the children had been put to bed, John said, 'It's time to go. It's all arranged. I am taking you to your Aunt in Budapest.'

* Postscript

When I had come home to Bratislava in September 1946, engaged to Bert, I was presented with the fact that I was an heiress. My grandfather's two houses in Pincehely in Hungary had been specifically bequeathed to me and I was the main beneficiary of my father's life insurance policy. I was getting married and going to England. Mother did not know that I had no intention of returning, ever, but the political situation had made a return highly unlikely anyway.

Not being able to come back did not mean the same as not intending to return. I went with Mother to the Public Notary to give her power of Attorney to deal with my inheritance from Father and Grandfather. I arranged to transfer my inheritance from Marton to Laci, his brother and from Gaspar to his sister and for Aunt Bella to have the rent from my houses in Pincehely.

Mother was going to send on my stuff to England. When the container arrived in the summer of 1947, I found that Mother had sent me not only my trousseau but also my share of the family inheritance; the silver cutlery and flatware which in our family was passed down to the eldest daughter. There were also wedding presents, among them the lapis lazuli and a gold Karlsbad dinner service which was a gift from the family and dozens of cut-glass crystal glasses as well as three antique Persian rugs. I had not known that Mother had asked Bert to send her the measurements of our bedroom and she had had a suite made from Canadian birds-eye maple. It was very modern, very Art Nouveau. She had thought it would be upsetting for me to sleep in the bed that had once belonged to Bert's first wife. Here she was right but I had already made other arrangements.

She also sent me a box of family photographs, pointers to a past that I did not wish to acknowledge. I consigned them to the attic, except for the photo of her and my father when they became engaged. Fabrics and materials were still very scarce and I marvelled how Mother had managed to obtain the mountains of bedding and bed linen as well as table linen and towels. There was so much table linen and of such good quality that my children and I still use some of it now and every item was embroidered with my initials.

Mother also packed in the trunk enough textiles for me to make clothes for many years to come. For this I was truly grateful, since clothing and fabrics were rationed in England. Remnants of these went into a large patchwork quilt I made for Chris, my son, which he calls his 'story telling quilt', because a story is attached to every patch. But then, we are story-telling people. Father told stories, I have written all my life, Chris and Pauline, my children, tell and write them and from infancy James, my grandson, has been using his vivid imagination to make up and tell tales galore. I had buried this part of my past successfully for many years but I have been told that the time has come to tell my story.

After all, I am old now and possibly the last of my generation. This book is not the whole story, just the beginning.

My life in Britain has been unusual and adventurous. This book was originally going to be called 'The Past Is Other Countries' and was not written for publication but for my children. It was to be followed by another book 'A Stranger In My New Country' about my experiences in Britain after 1947. Then, the synopsis of the story of *The Woman Without A Number* was chosen as a finalist in BBC television's *My Story* competition. The interviews and filming for that programme took me back to places I had never intended to revisit, in Germany and to Hungary, and opened up questions which, I felt, needed to be answered.

LEEDS 2010

If you enjoyed this, you'll love these from Scratching Shed Publishing Ltd...

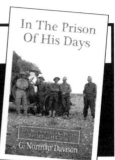

A sports autobiography like no other....

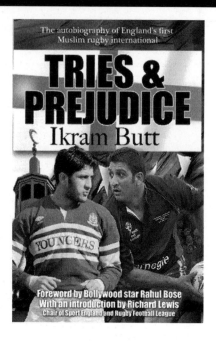

In February 1995, Ikram Butt became England's first Muslim rugby international in either code - blazing a trail for British Asians.

Since then, the former Leeds, Featherstone, London, Huddersfield and Hunslet rugby league star has continued to campaign for wider Asian involvement in sport and in 2004 was a prime mover in the formation of BARA - the British Asian Rugby Association. From the start, BARA had a vital social as well as sporting function. How could it not, in the wake of such 'War on Terror'-related atrocities as 9/11, 7/7 and the reported alienation of Britain's disaffected Asian youth?

Now, for the first time, Ikram Butt has his say, telling of his upbringing in Headingley; his own experiences on the wrong end of the law; the potential conflict between personal ambition and religion; racism in sport; run-ins with coaches and short-sighted officials; and, most recently, his regular visits to the House of Commons and pioneering development work in the UK, India and Pakistan.

Tries & Prejudice is by turns amusing, controversial, humane and eye-opening. It provides long overdue food for thought for politicians, the public and sports governing bodies alike.   ISBN 978-0956007537

Scratching Shed Publishing Ltd - Bringing history to life

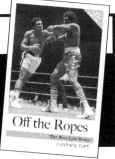

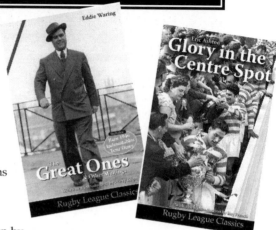

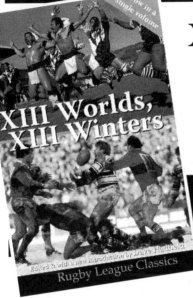

THE STORY OF FOOTBALL:
via the Moors, Dales and Wolds of England's largest and proudest county

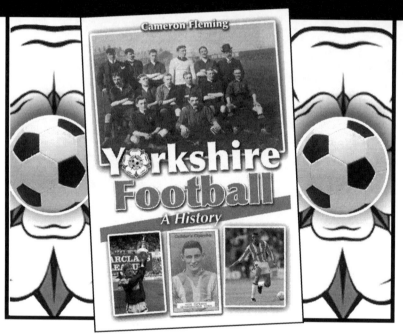

YORKSHIRE FOOTBALL
- A HISTORY
Cameron Fleming

ISBN: 978-0956252654

Scratching Shed Publishing Ltd

Stay up to date with all our lastest releases at
www.scratchingshedpublishing.co.uk

20409048R00164

Printed in Great Britain
by Amazon